TALKS for CHILDREN
on CHRISTIAN IDEALS

TALKS for CHILDREN
on CHRISTIAN IDEALS

Julius Fischbach

ABINGDON PRESS

NEW YORK
NASHVILLE

This book is affectionately dedicated
to

JOHN WILLIAM HEATER

our first grandson
whose mischievous twinkle, unbounded curiosity
and untiring energy symbolize for us
the lovable children everywhere
whom Jesus calls to himself

PREFACE

THE COMPLETION OF the manuscript of this book was done in La Canada, California, where we visited with our son Dave, his wife Pat, and our two grand-daughters, Cathy and Becky. While there we made a family tour of Disneyland and enjoyed the make-believe country where Tom Sawyer lives again, and Sleeping Beauty, Snow White and the Seven Dwarfs, Pinocchio, Mickey Mouse, and many other creatures of imagination come to objective reality through the magic of Walt Disney and his ingenious staff.

The day's experience was reassuring of the fact that old and young alike enjoy the storybook world brightened and enlivened by fancy. Although there were a few childless adults, the exploring of Disneyland was mainly a family excursion. As at the circus, the grown-ups who were there had one or more of the "small fry" along to explain their own presence.

Disneyland demonstrates that attention to the child is big business in America today. The juvenile trade is profitable financially, both in current dividends and in the promise of a future market. Industry and business find the child an eager and lucrative customer.

The Christian church should be the great sponsor of the child. Both by the admonition of Jesus—"Let the

7

children come to me"—and the hope of building the church of tomorrow, the directive is clear. Children need food, clothing, shelter, education, and entertainment, but most of all they need to know God and his will for their lives. The child should rightly be in the center of every church family, both in the graded program of education and in the united expressions of Christian worship and fellowship.

The thirty talks in this collection were prepared for the children of junior and primary age in our church and were told to them during the morning worship service. Remembering the many children we have been privileged to talk with about Christian ideals over the years, and anticipating many more such happy experiences, we send forth these story sermons to share with fellow lovers of boys and girls here, there, and everywhere.

JULIUS FISCHBACH

CONTENTS

FROM GREAT BIOGRAPHIES

FROM THE MISSION FIELD

FROM NATURE

TALKS FOR CHILDREN ON CHRISTIAN IDEALS

FROM THE JUNIOR CLASS

FROM THE CHANGING YEAR

TALKS for CHILDREN
on CHRISTIAN IDEALS

FROM GREAT
BIOGRAPHIES

* * *

1

A HELPLESS MAN WHO HELPED OTHERS

> *For the sake of Christ, then, I am content with weaknesses, insults, hardships, persecutions, and calamities; for when I am weak, then I am strong.* —II COR. 12:10

THE APOSTLE PAUL had some sort of illness which was very serious and caused him great trouble. Often he prayed to God to cure it. He called it a "thorn in the flesh" and asked God to remove it. God did not choose to take away the trouble but allowed Paul to suffer with it for his own good. At first Paul did not consider it good, but later, as he understood God's purpose, he gave thanks to God. He was not thankful for his suffering but thankful that through it he was led closer to the Lord.

This is what Paul said about it: "For the sake of

Christ, then, I am content with weaknesses, insults, hardships, persecutions, and calamities; for when I am weak, then I am strong." At another time, speaking of Christ's help, Paul said: "I can do all things in him who strengthens me."

What Paul learned, other men have learned through trouble and suffering. Paul was never helpless, though he was several times put into prison and was even chained in a dungeon.

Several years ago there was a man living in Australia who was actually helpless and yet was able, by Christ's help, to carry on a work that did good all around the world. This man was completely paralyzed, but he helped boys and girls in China, in Japan, in the Fiji Islands, in Ceylon, in Brazil, and in many other places. Does this sound impossible? Listen!

Robert Byers lived in a suburb of Adelaide, Australia. When we first hear of him he was an invalid, paralyzed from head to foot. He was not even able to feed himself. Someone else had to put food to his mouth for him to eat.

At first Robert Byers could see and hear as well as anyone. Gradually, however, the paralysis began to reach his eyes and his ears. Within a few years he was unable to see and his hearing became worse and worse until he was totally deaf.

This would seem to be just about as terrible a calamity as could happen to anyone. No doubt Robert Byers thought a great deal about his misfortune, and no one could have blamed him if he had even pitied himself. It seems, however, that he never did that. Even in his own suffering he was continually thinking of others.

Although he could neither see nor hear, he could still talk in a broken, stammering way. His mind was as active as ever, and he had been doing a lot of serious thinking about other people who, like himself, were paralyzed, or blind, or deaf. He wondered if there was anything he could do to cheer them up or help them in any way.

It may seem strange that a person who needed so much help himself should be always thinking of others and wondering how he could be of help to them. The very fact that his thoughts took this turn would indicate that he must have been trying to "think God's thoughts" rather than his own selfish ideas and attempting to allow God to use him for his own purposes.

A great idea came to Robert Byers. He told a friend who was visiting him one day, "There are many blind people, all around the world, and many of them are in great need. I have many friends, but some of these blind people have no friends at all. I will ask my friends to send me money as a birthday gift to use to help the blind, especially blind children. I will send this money where I think it will do the most good. I will try to find the most needy places in various parts of the world and send the money to help serve blind boys and girls in those places."

That was the plan, and it proved to be a great one. The friends liked the plan too and sent their money in such sums that soon it amounted to about $6,000 a year. Other friends had been doing some research and study. They

15

searched out the places where money was greatly needed to help minister to blind children.

Soon these places were decided upon, and the money was on its way. In a short time as many as eighty boys and girls in twenty-one different lands were being helped. The money was used for a hospital for blind children in India, for a hospital in Palestine, for a printing press using the Braille system in Japan, and for similar work for blind children in Ceylon, in China, in Fiji, in Brazil, and in many other parts of the world.

Of course, without the help of friends, Robert Byers could not have done this great work. These friends were a very important part of the program itself. The work needed to be done, and no one man could do it alone. Furthermore, no one man would live long enough to get it all accomplished.

Robert Byers died some years later, but because his friends had become so much interested in helping these blind children in so many parts of the world, the work went on. They formed an organization to continue in his memory. So not only did a helpless man help scores of others in need, but his concern caused a host of people to carry on this good work through the years and around the globe.

2

GEORGE WASHINGTON PREPARED FOR SERVICE

> *And Jesus increased in wisdom and in stature, and in favor with God and man.*
> —LUKE 2:52

THE LAST VERSE in the Gospel of Luke tells in one sentence the story of the growing experience of Jesus as a boy. We do not have details of these years of his life, but from Luke's account we learn that the boy Jesus lived a wholesome, normal life, well balanced in interests and activities. Some boys and girls spend so much time on special interests that they neglect other things just as important. God would have us to grow as Jesus did—physically, mentally, socially, and religiously. We call this the fourfold life.

When we read about the great leaders of our country, we sometimes find it difficult to learn very much about their childhood days. Because of this fact, myths or fables grow up to explain how even in early youth these great persons were learning the important lessons of life. Of course the truth is that important lessons were being learned, but the incidents that helped teach those lessons may never be known.

We know that George Washington, often referred to

as the "Father of Our Country," was truthful, honest, brave, fair-minded, and reverent. As a general of the army and as the first president of our country, he showed all these fine traits. His boyhood undoubtedly prepared him for his leadership in later life. Many stories are told about young George, but most of them are thought to be imaginary. There are some general facts which we can learn, however, and they help us to see how young George prepared himself for the important part he was later to play in the life of our nation.

We have often read of George's running, wrestling, climbing, swimming, and horseback riding. I remember seeing a name carved high up on the Natural Bridge in Virginia which is said to be George's carving. As you look at it, it seems impossible that any boy could have climbed up there and carved his name. Another story is about his throwing a dollar across the Potomac River. This, of course, could have been true. Rivers are not the same width all along their course. Farther up the stream the banks are close together, and a boy with a good arm could throw a rock or a dollar from bank to bank. The story about the cherry tree is probably a fable, but it does tell a true fact about George Washington, for he was honest and he was truthful.

It seems that George Washington, early in life, felt that he had a destiny to fulfill and wanted to prepare himself for it. The colony of Virginia was largely wilderness then, and much of the land to the west was unexplored. He saw the need of surveying the territory and learning how to cultivate the land. So as a school boy

18

he was especially interested in studying arithmetic, which is needed in civil engineering and surveying. He also learned all he could about better farming. He had been born on a farm, and after his father died his older half-brother Lawrence inherited the farm that has become known as Mount Vernon. George lived there with his brother for several years, and he saw the needs of the farmer or plantation owner.

Living in his brother's home, where many important people came from time to time, George learned the value of good manners. Historians have recorded many rules of good conduct which George copied out of the etiquette book because he wanted to remember them and use them. Some of them are

Keep your nails clean and short, also your hands and teeth clean, yet without showing any great concern for them.

Sleep not when others speak; sit not when others stand; speak not when you should hold your peace; walk not on when others stop.

In the presence of others, sing not to yourself with a humming noise, nor drum with your fingers or feet.

Turn not your back to others, especially in speaking; jog not the table or desk on which another reads or writes.

If others talk at table, be attentive but talk not with meat in your mouth.

Labor to keep alive in your breast that little spark of celestial fire called conscience.

George loved the out-of-doors and spent much of his time roaming through the woods and enjoying the beauty of hill and river, sky and land. He learned from the pioneers clearing away the trees to make fields, and became acquainted with the Indians who were wandering the forest paths. His great opportunity came when Lord Fairfax employed him to survey his large tracts of land. George had to travel many days through the forest and spend many nights under the stars. He learned how to take care of himself in the wilderness, and this knowledge served him later as he led the Continental Army as its commander in chief.

Visitors to Alexandria, Virginia, are shown a pew in Christ Church where George Washington sat as a worshiper. He was a religious man and was often in prayer. He felt the need for asking God to give him wisdom and strength to do his great task.

Although we do not know very much about George Washington as a boy, we know that he must have had high thoughts and dreamed bright dreams about the future. We are also sure that day by day he tried to get ready for his life service—in school, at home, and at work on the plantation. He was prepared for each important commission as it came, and he did each task well—which is the best way of preparing oneself for something greater.

George Washington was a great and trusted leader in his manhood because he spent his boyhood in training for the future.

3

ONLY THE BEST IS GOOD ENOUGH

And God saw everything that he had made,
and behold, it was very good. —GEN. 1:31

THE FIRST CHAPTER of Genesis tells the wonderful story of God's creation of the world and animal and human life. At the close of that chapter, in the very last verse, there is a phrase that should be a challenge to all of us. As God's children we should never be satisfied with anything less than our very best efforts when we are given something to do. It has been said: "Anything that is worth doing is worth doing well." The verse in Genesis says: "God saw everything that he had made, and behold, it was very good." God's creative work was perfect.

It is not so important where a person lives. It makes no difference what type of work he does if he has ability in that line. The things that count are *how* he does his work and *why*. A good workman is one who does the best he is able to do because he wants to please God.

More than two hundred years ago an old man lived and worked in a remote village in Italy. So far as we know he never lived in any other city and did very little traveling away from home. But he became known as the most skillful workman in his craft in the whole world, and in all history.

His name was Antonio Stradivari, and his business was violin making. Actually, very little is known of Antonio, but his violins and cellos are so beautiful and so wonderfully made that they are considered priceless treasures. Every instrument that Antonio made sang his praise, and he is said to have made about fifteen hundred of them.

It is also said that each of Antonio's instruments was different. No two were just alike in appearance or in tone. People who are authorities on stringed instruments say that Antonio's violins and cellos have "personality." In other words, they are like people. Each is an individual, not just another instrument.

This is why his violins have names. Some of them are the "Messiah," the "Tuscan," the "Paganini," the "Betts," the "Dolphin," the "Boissier," and the "Cessot."

Antonio was commissioned to make violins and cellos for great persons in different parts of the world. He made a complete set of instruments for the king of England. Six violins were made for the king of Spain and twelve for the elector of Poland.

Why should one man's violins be better than those made by any other man? Antonio had pupils whom he taught to make good violins, but none of them could make a violin as fine as their teacher's. Since Antonio's death many careful workmen have taken the exact measurements of his instruments and tried to copy them, but none has succeeded in making a violin with the wonderful tone quality of a Stradivarius.

It is necessary to study Antonio in his workshop to understand his unusual ability. We need to see how he worked and how long and patiently he kept working. He actually tried to make each violin as nearly perfect as it was possible for him to make it. When he was sure that it was the very best he could do at that time, he put his mark on it—a Maltese cross in a double circle with the initials "A.S."

Antonio was never satisfied. He always felt he could do better. So he would carefully select the finest pieces of maple and pine wood and try again to do a better job. He studied the pieces of wood to discover how to put them together to produce the best sound. Then he varnished his completed instrument with a varnish made by a secret formula which was perfect for his violins. No one has ever been able to discover how to make this particular kind of varnish.

It seems that, all his life, Antonio kept learning more and more about building better instruments. The violin which judges of such instruments claim is the very best of all the fine violins he made is called the "Alard." It was made in 1715, when Antonio was seventy-one years old. The very best cello is called the "Piatti" and was made in 1720, when he was seventy-six years old. In fact, Antonio kept making violins until within a year of his death and he lived to be ninety-three.

Perhaps someday you will have an opportunity to see and hear some of the violins and cellos Antonio Stradivari made. If you ever go to Washington, D. C., be sure to visit the Library of Congress. There, in a glass case, you will see the Stradivari Memorial—three violins, one viola, and one cello. You may even be fortunate enough to hear them played, for when great artists come to Washington they often give concerts in the concert hall of the library and play these famous instruments. There is no finer treat for one who loves and understands music than to hear a truly great artist play a Stradivari violin.

Not only have musicians fallen in love with Antonio's violins, but poets have been inspired to write about them. The most famous bit of verse is by George Eliot. Her poem sums up the genius of this great artisan in a very few lines, but these lines stretch our imaginations to see right into the workshop of Antonio and give a clue to the secret of his greatness:

> 'Tis God gives skill,
> But not without men's hands: he could not make
> Antonio Stradivari's violins
>   Without Antonio . . .

4

A BLIND WOMAN WHO SEES

> Having the eyes of your hearts enlight-
> ened . . .   —EPH. 1:18

ALMOST EVERYONE has heard the name Helen
Keller. I say "almost" because there is no name known
by all people everywhere. Even the name of Christ must
be carried by the missionaries to distant lands, for many
have never heard that name which is so precious to us.

Although you have heard the name Helen Keller,
there are many things you may not know about her. She
is blind, yet she can see. She is deaf, yet she can hear. She
has never heard anyone's voice—not even her own—yet
she can talk. She frequently speaks to large audiences.

You see, Helen Keller began life with three great handicaps. She was blind and completely deaf at the age of
nineteen months. She lived in a world of darkness and
silence. Because she could not hear, no one could speak
to her, and she could not learn to talk.

Then an unusual thing happened. A young woman
named Anne Sullivan came to be Helen's nurse and
teacher when Helen was four years of age. How could she
possibly teach a little girl who could neither see nor
hear? How could you tell such a child anything, and how
could you know if she got your message?

It was a big problem, but Miss Sullivan found a way. She began by pressing her fingers on Helen's hand. She worked out a code by touch. It must have taken a long time for Helen even to get the idea that Miss Sullivan was trying to talk to her. Although she was sitting by her teacher's side, she was as far away as if she were at the bottom of a deep well with the top tightly sealed. But the message finally got through to Helen, and she and Miss Sullivan began "talking" to each other.

Helen was a bright girl with a good mind. In just a few weeks she was beginning to be able to make signs and signals to Miss Sullivan, and they were able to understand each other.

It is a long story and an amazing one. Miss Keller learned to read Braille, which is the raised-dot system by which the blind read with their fingers. She went through the courses of grade school. Then she went to high school and to college. Of course Miss Sullivan went with her to help her with her studies. Helen Keller not only completed her college work, but she was graduated with high honors at the head of her class.

When Helen Keller finished her college work, she wanted to find her place of usefulness in the world. You might ask, How could a person so handicapped find work to do? Actually her great opportunity came because of her handicaps. She said to herself: "There are thousands of children and young people who are blind like me. I can be of help to them." That is exactly what she decided to do. She determined to help others who were blind. She wrote to them on her Braille typewriter. She talked with them and encouraged them. She helped them to have faith in themselves and to study and work as she had done.

Miss Keller was so successful in helping other blind people that her work grew larger and larger. She was invited to go to distant lands to help the blind. An organization called the American Foundation for the Blind was formed. Miss Keller was made the counselor on national and international relations. In her work today she travels all over the world. She has been to most of the European countries, Japan, Korea, Africa, New Zealand, and Australia. In fact, there are few countries in the world which Miss Keller has not visited. Everywhere she goes she inspires all who meet her. She has written several books, and her life is the subject of two interesting movies. She is truly a missionary of God's good will and love to all people.

Helen Keller helps us understand a text found in the first chapter of Ephesians. Paul refers to the "eyes of the heart." He says, "Having the eyes of your hearts enlightened, that you may know what is the hope to which he has called you . . ."

Some time ago a reporter visited Miss Keller at her home in Westport, Connecticut. He found her in her beautiful rose garden. He wondered how she could enjoy a garden without being able to see the flowers. But, she told him, she could see the beautiful roses. She said, "It is wonderful to have eyes and ears in one's soul; it completes the glory of living."

Miss Keller sees with inner sight. Speaking of the sky

27

at night, she said, "I cannot see the stars you see in the heavens, but there are other stars just as bright that shine in my soul."

She feels her roses and loves them one by one. She has learned how to enjoy the warmth of the sunshine and the brushing touch of the wind. She loves God and feels that he is always near her. She looks at her very troubles as invitations to great adventure. Because she is blind and deaf she has a wonderful feeling of friendship with all people in the world, of all races and nations, who also are blind or deaf.

Helen Keller is God's ambassador of good will, friendship, and hope to all who live in darkness and solitude. She is what Jesus called a "light" in the world.

* * *

5

YOU CAN DO IT!

> I can do all things in him who strengthens
> me.   —PHIL. 4:13

WE THINK of the apostle Paul as one of the greatest saints and one of the best Christian preachers who ever lived. Life for him was not easy, however. In fact, few men have had as much to suffer and as much to overcome as he did. Listen to his story: "Five times I have received at the hands of the Jews the forty lashes less one. Three times I have been beaten with rods; once I was stoned. Three times I have been shipwrecked; a night and a day I have been adrift at sea." He continues to tell about dangers from robbers and dangers at sea and in the wilderness as well as great suffering from hunger and thirst.

But Paul had a secret of success. He was able to overcome all difficulties. He put it into one sentence: "I can do all things in him who strengthens me."

No one knows what any boy or girl can do or become until that boy or girl has given God a chance.

Have you heard the story of Steve Pigott? Steve was the son of an Irishman who had come to this country and settled. The father's name was Pat Pigott. He could neither read nor write. He did not want his son Steve to go to school, for he thought it was a waste of time. Pat needed Steve to help him work on the farm.

At high school Steve had a teacher who believed in him and urged him to study and complete his high-school course. One day this teacher said to Steve, "What would you like to be?"

Steve knew, for he had thought about it a great deal; but he doubted if he could ever become what he dreamed about, because it required a lot of training. He said: "I'd like to be a marine engineer."

Instantly the teacher said: "You can be one, Steve. I know you can. All you need is to try—hard."

Steve was accustomed to hard work. Every morning he got up long before sunrise. He had many chores to do before breakfast. After school he went home and worked hard until dark, for there is lots to be done on a farm. He did not have time for many of the sports and fun other boys enjoyed. It seemed that all Steve knew was work, but he did not mind it, because he knew what he wanted and was willing to pay the price for it.

Steve kept working at his studies and finished his high-school course. Then, even though his father thought it was not worth while, he enrolled in the engineering school at Columbia University. To stay there he had to pay his own tuition and room and board. He got a job in a streetcar barn, cleaning the cars and getting them ready for the next day's run.

Although it took hard work and long hours to put himself through the university, Steve kept going. Finally he was graduated. On the day he received his diploma he received a telegram from his high-school teacher. It contained just four words: "I told you so." That was a short message but it said a lot. Steve's teacher was confident he would make good.

Five years later Steve Pigott went to Scotland to install an engine in a newly built ship. He expected to come home as soon as this was finished. The company for which he did the engine job liked his work and asked him to stay on and work for them.

Steve kept changing his plans about coming home to America. One job led to another, and he designed machinery and worked on ship after ship in Scotland, until, at last, he decided to make Scotland his home.

Would you like to know the names of some of the ships Steve Pigott helped to build and send out on the high seas? One of them was the battleship "Hood." Another was the great passenger liner "Queen Mary." The largest of Steve's ships was one of the greatest liners ever built, the "Queen Elizabeth."

After all this accomplishment, and in recognition of his fine work, Steve Pigott received one of the highest honors to be given to a person in the British Empire. He was knighted and became Sir Stephen Pigott.

When the news of Steve's title was reported in this country, a newspaperman hunted up the high-school teacher who had urged Steve to be what he wanted to be. The reporter found his former teacher and talked with her about Steve. She said, "I knew Steve could be whatever he wanted to be if only he believed in himself and did his best."

Yes, the teacher was right when she said, "Steve, you can do it." Steve proved she was right by becoming one of the world's greatest marine engineers.

* * *

6

NOT AFRAID TO BE AFRAID

> *And I was with you in weakness and in much*
> *fear and trembling.* —I COR. 2:3

THE APOSTLE PAUL was no coward. He had some terrible experiences. Once he was stoned and left for dead, several times he was put into prison, and three times he was beaten by the soldiers. None of these things kept him from going on with his work of preaching and teaching. He was not afraid of any man. But he did write to the Corinthians that when he came to preach to them he came "in weakness and in much fear and trembling."

Was Paul afraid to speak in public? Was he trembling because he feared that people would laugh at him? No. Paul was afraid only of failing to win men to Christ. He was afraid he would not be persuasive enough to get them to listen to him tell the gospel story. He was afraid some might be lost. He was deeply concerned about all people. He wanted all to know God's love. He trembled as he thought of the possibility of some refusing to listen and turning their backs on God.

Years ago, in the mountain country, there was a man whom people feared. He did not look like other people. He let his hair and beard grow long. He wore ragged clothes and a hat with the brim pulled down so low you could scarcely see his eyes.

When "Wild" Walt came to town everyone stayed at a distance. Persons who saw him in time would cross over to the other side of the street and watch him out of the corners of their eyes. He did not like to have people staring at him, and if he caught them doing so, he would "tell them off" with loud words. Dogs barked at Wild Walt and children ran home when they heard he was in town.

Of course this peculiar man had to come to town occasionally to buy groceries, and when he did so, the other customers were very willing to let him have all the room he wanted. Usually they went outside the store until he had finished his shopping. He caused no trouble with the storekeeper. He simply asked for what he wanted, gave the grocer some dirty money out of a worn leather pouch he carried tied to his belt, and went his way. One purchase he always made was shells for his long-barreled shot gun. He hunted a great deal and was often seen striding along with his gun on his shoulder.

One thing everyone knew about Wild Walt—he did not like the church or church people. Once when a special meeting was being held in the church just down the hill from the little shack where he lived, he did a terrible thing. He came out on his porch and yelled threats in the direction of the church, demanding that they "stop all that noise!" Of course the people were just singing, and they were probably singing loud enough to be heard all over town. They really felt like praising God for his many blessings, and they were glad to let their fellow citizens share their happiness. Christian people sing not only to tell God their love but to let the whole world know as well.

When the singing continued (for the people inside the church could not even hear Wild Walt shouting), Walt went into the house and got his gun. He aimed at the tower of the church and pulled the trigger. Some of the shot hit the church bell and made it ring out. Everyone in town heard the loud explosion. No one was hurt but it is against the law to do such a thing as Walt did, and the police were very soon heading his way. Walt was

33

arrested and put in jail for several days to "cool off," as the judge said.

After Walt was released from jail and had returned to his shack on the hill, the minister of the church determined to pay him a call. When his congregation heard of it, they were shocked. Quite a number of them came to the parsonage and urged their pastor not to go to see this wild man. They were afraid their pastor would be shot or hurt in some serious way.

But the minister could not be influenced to change his plan. He was going to see Wild Walt that very afternoon. So up the hill he went, with a good part of the townspeople watching him from the streets and from their windows. All were sure that trouble would start as soon as the preacher knocked on the door of the shack and, together, they were ready to rush to his rescue.

The minister, without a moment's hesitation, walked up the boardwalk, went up on the porch, and stood in front of the door, knocking.

To the horror of the waiting people below, Wild Walt opened the door and stood there with his gun in his hands, looking defiantly at the preacher. For a long time he stood blocking the doorway. Then, as the people watched, he laid down his gun and stood aside as the minister walked into the house.

For a long time the people waited. Up on the hill all was still. What had happened to their preacher? Was he safe? Was Wild Walt up to some trick? These were anxious minutes.

Finally the door opened, and the preacher and Walt

34

came out on the porch. To the amazement of all they shook hands and Walt put his hand on the minister's shoulder and smiled at him. Then he stood waving at him as he went down the walk and back down the hill.

It was a long story the preacher had to tell to his congregation. He found that Walt was a man who needed a friend. He thought no one cared for him and this is what had made him so peculiar. He was just waiting for someone to care enough to speak to him; to treat him like a human being. When his mother died many years ago, Walt thought even God had stopped loving him. He had brooded over his sorrow so much he had become bad-tempered and gruff, and his own behavior caused other people to stay away from him. He did not want to be such an unwanted person but did not know how to be different.

The preacher said he was sure Walt would be in the service next Sunday morning, because he was going up to his house and bring him down. Walt had asked him if he would be kind enough to go with him to church. The man had not been inside a church for thirty years and was afraid to go alone!

When the people of the congregation asked their preacher if he had been afraid as he went up the hill to Wild Walt's house, he said; "Yes, I must admit I was afraid. I was afraid he would not let me in or listen to me. I was afraid I might fail to win him; but I knew he needed Christ just as much as all of us do. I had no fear of failure if only he would allow Christ to come in with me."

FROM THE
MISSION FIELD

* * *

7

LEARNING TO MAKE PLOWS FROM SWORDS

And they shall beat their swords into plowshares,
and their spears into pruning hooks;
nation shall not lift up sword against nation,
neither shall they learn war any more.
—ISA. 2:4

THREE OF THE Old Testament prophets, when
they talked about the hope of peace on earth among the
nations, used an expression about swords and plows. Of
course, the sword is an instrument of war, and the plow
is an instrument of peace. So when they dreamed of the
time when men would not fight wars any more, these
prophets said the swords would be beaten into plowshares. Since the steel in the sword would not be used for
fighting, it could be put into the furnace or on the
anvil and shaped into a blade for a plow.

When the prophets spoke about plows and swords,

they meant all the instruments of peace and all the instruments of war. Soldiers in modern days do not fight with swords. Instead of swords they use machine guns and tanks, long-muzzled cannon and—most terrible of all—atom bombs and missiles. Neither do they ride on horses as soldiers once did. They ride in fast jets and great bomber planes.

There are changes, too, in the plow and the growing of crops on the farm. You do not see horses pulling plows very often today. There are tractors and all kinds of cultivating machines. There are also harvesting machines that do automatically what was once done by hand.

So when we think of the prophets' words today, we want peace and brotherhood just as much as they did, but peace and good will are brought about in new ways. Did you ever think of a school or college as a "plowshare"? Most colleges have nothing to do with farms and the growing of crops, but some do. Agricultural colleges teach young people to be better farmers. But all good colleges and universities, as well as grade schools and high schools, should be teaching boys and girls and young people to be better citizens. Being better citizens means not only being good neighbors with the people who live on your street, but also being helpful and neighborly with all people on all the streets in all the cities and villages around the globe. This is "plowing for peace."

When we think of it in that way, then a good college, especially a Christian college or university, is a splendid

37

kind of "plowshare." It is helping its students prepare their minds to think peace. It is planting seeds of good will and brotherhood and cultivating kind thoughts toward people of all races and nations.

In the city of Tokyo, Japan, there is a university which is really doing today what the prophets talked about yesterday—beating swords into plowshares.

You may ask, Why is this particular university doing this more than any other university? That is a good question, and there is a most interesting answer. During World War II one of the most deadly war planes that flew was the Japanese fighter plane called the "Zero." It was made in a factory in Tokyo. This factory built thousands of these fast planes, and young Japanese air corps men flew them. These Zeros were the modern "swords" of the Japanese army.

When the war was over and Japan was defeated, the factory which had built the Zero planes was closed down. Of course it could have been used to make some kind of useful machine such as automobiles, trucks, or washing machines. But something much better than this happened.

Some men and women of good will in Japan, working together with men and women of good will in America, thought of a wonderful idea. They said, "We will tear down the old Zero factory and, on the same spot, build something really fine. On the ground where this war factory once stood, we will build a great university—a Christian university—and there we will teach young people to be brothers and sisters to all the world."

38

That is exactly what they did. The people of Japan bought the 365 acres where the war factory stood and dedicated it to education. Christian leaders in America joined with them to build the International Christian University. Today this Christian university is proving to be a great dynamo of peace and brotherhood. On the very spot where the war factory once stood, young people of many nationalities are today studying to be intelligent and useful world citizens. Two languages are used in the university—Japanese and English. The teachers are all carefully chosen Christian scholars. The campus is a community of good neighbors. International Christian University is truly God's farm, being plowed and cultivated to grow the fruits of international good will.

So today, as we read the prophets' words that tell their dream of the future in terms of swords beaten into plowshares, we can point to the International Christian University and say; "Here is one good way to plow for the Prince of Peace."

8

THE GOOD SAMARITAN JEEP

> He had compassion, and went to him and
> bound up his wounds, pouring on oil and wine;
> then he set him on his own beast and brought
> him to an inn, and took care of him.
>
> —LUKE 10:33-34

JERRY IS A jeep—but not an ordinary jeep. Jerry
is a missionary jeep, though he was not always a missionary. In fact, he arrived in the Philippine Islands with the
United States Army. During World War II he was a
military jeep and carried soldiers to the front. He also
sometimes carried wounded men to the hospital. But
that was a long time ago. After the war was over, some
missionaries saw how useful a jeep could be and bought
Jerry for the use of the mission station in Roxas City,
Panay Island.

Jerry is not a very fancy automobile. In fact, he is
rather dilapidated. One of his doors sags on its hinges
and must be held shut by a rope tied through holes made
by machine gun bullets long ago. The latch is gone. The
seats are worn, and many torn places allow the wadding
inside to poke out. The springs are stiff and make riding
very rough indeed. The tires are old and have been

patched so often they are likely to blow out or let down almost any time and anywhere.

But with all his weak spots Jerry is a much-loved jeep. He is rough-riding and old, but he is always ready to do his part and never groans or complains. He goes bouncing over the roads, with all four cylinders pounding away and all four wheels pulling. No hill is too steep for him, no mud too sticky, and no rut too deep. He enjoys his work—and why shouldn't he? He is busy all day long helping the missionaries bring good cheer to others.

If Jerry has a memory—and I doubt if he has—he might think of the time when he rushed out to a bamboo hut far away to the north, on a road that was only a trail through the swamp. He went there to get a very sick boy and bring him to the hospital. When the doctor received the boy at the hospital, he was too sick even to say "thank you" for the ride. Later, however, when Jerry took him back home to his mother, he was well and happy and just couldn't say "thank you" enough. He enjoyed the bouncy road and reached out to try to touch the long leaves of the banana trees by the roadside. He imitated the calls of the parrots as they greeted the jeep with their shrill cries. He had a wonderful time on that trip back to the bamboo hut he called home.

Jerry might also have recalled the fun he had had many times with the Four-H boys and girls. He had taken groups of them on trips and picnics. How they would crowd into Jerry's seats! The seats were not enough to hold them. Always one or two insisted on riding "pony back" on the hood. This was never allowed until they

41

were near their destination, and then the driver would go very slowly so the riders would not be bounced off. But these boys and girls were lots of fun, and Jerry was always happy when it was his turn to take them for a ride.

Jerry not only carried boys and girls, their fathers and mothers, and the missionaries; he also often carried freight. That is, he carried boxes, piled high. What was in them he did not always know, but from the conversation he learned a lot. Jerry never talked, and because he kept still, he heard a lot and knew a great deal about the work of the mission station. For instance, one day he worked all day, carrying boxes of supplies for the hospital. They had come all the way from America. There were sheets and pillowcases for the cots, bandages and tape, many kinds of medicine in bottles, and some instruments which the doctors and nurses were to use. Jerry did not understand much about such things, so he did not know what kinds of instruments they were.

Jerry often carried food. Many times it was necessary to take vegetables and flour or meal far out into the back country to give to families who were in need of something to eat. He also carried seeds to farmers and—believe it or not—he had carried live pigs and chickens too. These were very special pigs and chickens. Some of the farmers who received them called them "Christian" pigs and chickens. You see, they were pigs and chickens of good breeds to replace the poor kinds which the farmers had. Their pigs and chickens could scarcely keep themselves alive, they were so lanky and weak. These "Christian" pigs and chickens were from the best stock the missionaries could get from America. They were big and strong. With the new stock the Filipino farmers could raise whole herds of pigs and flocks of chickens of the good varieties.

Jesus once told a story about a poor man who was robbed and left dying by the roadside. A good Samaritan happened to come along that way, and he proved to be a good neighbor to the dying man. The Samaritan not only bound up the man's wounds but he put him on his donkey and took him to an inn where he could be cared for. Perhaps Jerry has never heard this story, but we who have heard it may think of Jerry himself as a good Samaritan helping the missionaries to minister to needy people in the name of Christ.

* * *

9

THE YOUNGEST MISSIONARY

> Let your light so shine before men, that they
> may see your good works and give glory to your
> Father who is in heaven. —MATT. 5:16

DEBBIE WAS only six years old but she was a missionary. Yes, she was a missionary of Christ in the faraway land of Burma.

Now this does not mean that all by herself Debbie had boarded a ship and sailed away to Burma to tell the boys and girls of that distant land about Jesus. You see, her father and mother were missionaries, and she was born in the great city of Rangoon. She was really a missionary even before she started to school, but it was at the beginning of her school days that she knew how important a missionary's life can be.

Debbie's school was not like yours. She was an American girl going to school in a foreign country. Her classmates were all brown-skinned boys and girls, wearing clothes very different from the clothes you and your schoolmates wear. The parents of some of the children were Karens, some were Chinese, and many were Burmese. Two languages were used in the school—Burmese and English. So Debbie was learning to speak and read Burmese as well as English.

Debbie was different from the other children. She dressed as they did and she was learning to speak Burmese as they did. But her skin was white, and her parents were Christians, not Buddhists.

Most of the people who live in Burma are Buddhists. The great Shwe Dagon pagoda is in Rangoon. Its high dome and spire reach up so high you can see its gold glistening in the sun for many miles around. There are many other temples and pagodas throughout the land. The Christians are few in Burma, and the Buddhists are many.

Debbie was a "foreigner" in the land in which she lived. Because she was different in color of skin and different in family and religion, the other boys and girls sometimes tried to have fun at her expense. No one likes to be laughed at. It is hard to keep from being angry and talking back when such things happen.

Debbie's father and mother were very wise missionaries as well as very loving parents. They told Debbie before she went to school the very first day: "Some of the other children may make fun of you and call you names. You may not like it at all; but remember that you are a missionary just as we are. This is your chance to show the other boys and girls how a Christian acts. Do not get angry. Do not talk back or strike anyone. Just smile and go your way without causing any trouble. After a while the rest of the students will know they cannot bother you, and they will respect you and love you for being friendly and acting as a good neighbor should."

Debbie thought about these words as she went to school that first day. She was not a total stranger, for some of her playmates were in the same class. Most of the children, however, were new to her. She was very quiet, since she was just a little afraid of what might happen. She did not want to be disliked, and she did not want to be laughed at.

Debbie studied hard, for she wanted to learn and she wanted to be a good pupil. But it was not many days until some of the girls pointed at her as they walked toward home after school was out. They asked if she was scared, because her face was so pale. She just smiled and said she would be scared if she did not know her lesson, and they all laughed.

Several times after that she was pointed out and talked about. The children even made up a little song and sang about her, but Debbie smiled and soon they stopped the song because they saw it did not make any difference with Debbie. She just attended to her own business as she walked along with the girls who lived in her neighborhood.

Then one Saturday night at the supper table Debbie said, "Daddy, can we drive the car around to Ma Hla Thene's house in the morning and take her with us to Sunday school?"

"Why, of course," said Daddy, "but are you sure her father will let Ma Hla Thene go with us? You know he is a very strict Buddhist."

"I'm sure it will be all right," said Debbie. "I was in Ma Hla Thene's home today and talked with her father. He said he would be glad to have her go with me to my Sunday school if she wanted to. He even said he would like to go too sometime."

That was a few years ago, when Debbie was in the first grade. She proved that she was a missionary, and a good one. Ma Hla Thene was the first classmate she invited to her Sunday school, but many others have been invited since. Not only did Ma Hla Thene come but after a few weeks she brought all her family with her. They liked Debbie's Sunday school so much that they came Sunday after Sunday. Later, when Debbie's father had a class for all who wanted to know the meaning of the Christian religion, Ma Hla Thene, her mother, her father, and her brother all attended. When the class

46

was finished, they were baptized and became members of Debbie's church.

Debbie continues to smile and sing and to invite her friends to her church. She wants them to learn about Jesus and the Christian way of life. She is trying to be the kind of person Jesus was talking about when he said, "Let your light so shine before men, that they may see your good works and give glory to your Father who is in heaven."

* * *

10

A STRANGE TELEGRAM

> Honor your father and your mother, that your days may be long in the land which the Lord your God gives you. —EXOD. 20:12

THE MISSIONARY from Assam was telling about his work in that distant country in the northern part of India. If you point directly to it on the other side of the globe, you will find that it is almost straight down from where you live. He told of the tea gardens there where many thousands of coolies work. He said that these tea gardens or plantations are very lovely to see. The tea plants are bushes growing in great fields in the midst of trees, for they are planted in a grove. These trees shade the tea plants so the sun will not cause them to burn and die. Each day the girls who pick the tea go through the plantation with large baskets on their heads. They pinch off the end of the tea branch—two leaves and a bud—and pitch it up into the basket. When the baskets are filled with leaves, the men carry them to trucks and haul them to the sheds where they are dried and processed for the market.

Back in the jungle may be found men working at another kind of job. They are stalking wild animals. They are hunters who catch animals for zoos all over the world. In these jungles are wild elephants, tigers, leopards, and bears. There are also herds of rhinoceroses and buffalo, and smaller animals—jackals, foxes, goats, and deer. The most venomous snake of the world is found here too—the deadly cobra.

The most dangerous of all the inhabitants of this wild country, however, are the wild men of the Naga and Garo hills. Many thousands of these people have been won by the missionaries. They have become Christians and have changed their terrible ways. But the wild men of the hills were once head-hunters. The missionary said that the greatest miracle to be seen anywhere on the mission field is the change that has made gentle men and women of the head-hunters in Assam.

After telling about these unusual things, the missionary told a story which was of special interest to the boys and girls. He said, "Did you ever hear of a telegram without words? Did you ever see a telegram that could not be written down?"

The story of the strange telegram came from the very northern part of the country of Assam, up at Sadiya. That is the town which our air force men knew during World War II. It was the place from which the pilots took off when they "flew the hump," over the lofty Himalaya Mountains into China.

The missionary was teaching a school in Sadiya, and many native boys were in his classes. One day one of the boys came to him and said: "Please, sir, let me be excused from my classes. I have just received a telegram from my father, and I must go home at once."

The missionary could not understand such a telegram. There were no telegraph wires in that part of the world. There were no telephones and no way to send a message by wire even if one wished to do so.

"You know there is no telegraph station here," said the missionary.

"But the message was brought to me this morning," said the boy.

"Even if a telegram could be sent, your father could not send one, for he can neither write nor read," continued the missionary.

"But I have the telegram here in my hand," said the boy.

"Let me see your telegram then," said the missionary.

And what a telegram it was! the boy held up a pouch made of dry grass and reeds. Inside were a rock and a dried red pepper.

"So that is your telegram. What does it say?" asked the missionary.

"I can read it easily," said the boy. "It says, 'My heart is heavy, Son, and unless you come at once, it will be bitter.' The rock tells me that my father's heart is sorrowful. The dried pepper tells me he is in great need of my help and that I must hurry to get there in time."

Of course, the missionary allowed the boy to leave the school and go to his father as fast as he could travel. A father loves his son in Assam just as a father loves his son in the United States, or in Mexico, or in any other part of the world. And in Assam a son can comfort and help his father when he is in need of him just as boys do in America or anywhere else.

The missionary thought of the fifth commandment, which tells us we should honor our fathers and our mothers. He was glad that this boy loved his father and honored him enough to want to leave his school and all the other boys in the mission station and travel the many weary miles on foot to help his father in his time of trouble.

The missionary thought of his own father and his own days away from home when he went to a distant town to attend college, and he said to himself: "Father love does not know race, nation, or color. Fathers and sons need each other whether they be in the jungle or in the city. It is a fine thing to see a young man who can hear his father call from many miles distant. It is still finer to hear that son answer, 'Yes, I hear you, Father. I'm coming at once.'"

11

OUTCASTS ARE INSIDE!

> The blind receive their sight and the lame
> walk, lepers are cleansed and the deaf hear, and
> the dead are raised up, and the poor have good
> news preached to them.   —MATT. 11:5

As WE READ the story of the life of Jesus, we
learn that among the sick people whom he healed were
some with leprosy. This disease is not common in our
part of the world, and even the doctors in America are
not familiar with it. It was a common disease in Jesus'
day in Palestine, and it is still found in Oriental countries.

In connection with the disease of leprosy, the word
"unclean" is used. In earlier days those who suffered
from leprosy were called unclean because the disease
was considered incurable. It was also thought the disease
was contagious. A person having leprosy was required to
stay at a distance from other people. In fact, the law required that lepers should not live inside the city or town
with other people. They must stay outside the city walls.
Often a number of lepers would live together in the
fields outside the city. Since they were not well and were
not strong enough to work, they begged at the city gate
or at the side of the road.

51

In the eighth chapter of Matthew we are told of a leper whom Jesus met. Jesus had been preaching on the mountain. When he came down into the valley, a leper came to him and knelt before him, asking to be made well. Jesus answered his request and healed him. On another occasion, when Jesus was walking through Samaria, ten lepers came to meet him. They stood at a distance and begged him to have mercy on them. Jesus healed them all, but only one showed that he was grateful by coming back to thank Jesus for his kind act.

Up in Jorhat, Assam, there is a very unusual village. Its citizens are all lepers. It is not just a village, however. It is a Christian community. Each family has a bamboo house and a small yard. There is a school for the children, and there are garden plots and small shops where men and women work. The gardens grow pineapples and vegetables which are sold in the village of Jorhat. In the shops, mats are made of palm-leaf strips, and cloth is made of silk thread. The thread itself is spun from the cocoons of the silkworms.

There is an interesting story back of this leper village. In fact, there could have been no leper village without friends to buy the land, build the houses, and invite the people to come to live there. Lepers are poor people. They are not able to make a living without the help of others.

The friends who made this village possible are the Christian missionaries. Because they love all people, lepers are included too. Because lepers are outcasts and homeless, the missionaries have built them homes and invited them to come, in the name of Christ.

From what we have said about leprosy, you might expect lepers to be very sorrowful, unhappy people. They are, unless they have friends who care for them and help them. The lepers who live in the leper village are happy. They are proud of their little houses. They sing as they work in their gardens. They smile as visitors come to see their village. They not only have food to eat and clothes to wear, but they have hope of being cured of their leprosy. You see, some of their missionary friends are doctors; these doctors visit them, give them medicine, and treat their disease. Not all cases can be cured. Many of the lepers can only be comforted and relieved of some of their pain. But many can be cured if their disease has not gone too far. The children of leper fathers and mothers are protected against catching the disease.

Until Christians befriended the lepers, they had no friends at all. Other people were afraid of their disease, and none cared to risk being around them. But Christian missionaries have shown the spirit of Christ in ministering to them in their great need.

Once when Jesus was going from place to place preaching, that great wilderness preacher, John the Baptist, was in prison. He heard about the great deeds of Jesus. He was lonely and sorrowful. He had believed that Jesus was the Christ, but now he was so dejected that he began to wonder. So he sent a messenger to ask Jesus if he really was the Christ. Jesus sent this message back

53

to him, "Go and tell John what you hear and see: the blind receive their sight and the lame walk, lepers are cleansed and the deaf hear."

Is it not true that the kindness of the missionaries in ministering to the lepers, whom others shun, is good evidence that they too have the spirit of the Christ?

* * *

12

LOOK IN THE BIBLE MIRROR

> For if any one is a hearer of the word and not a doer, he is like a man who observes his natural face in a mirror. . . But he who looks into the perfect law. . . and perseveres. . . shall be blessed In his doing.—JAS. 1:23-25

THE MISSIONARY FROM Burma was telling the children about some of the unusual customs of that interesting land beyond the sea. He said the Burmese believe in spirits—both good and evil. They believe there are thousands of them around. They believe also that these spirits affect their lives and either help or hurt them.

In Thailand and in Burma the people set up little spirit houses in their yards and in their stores. These look very much like birdhouses. They are about the same size, though usually more fancy and ornamental. Often they are painted bright colors and are very attractive. Each day the believer in spirits will put an offering by the spirit house. It may be a serving of rice, or a banana, or a bunch of flowers. He thinks this offering will cause the spirit to be kind to him. If he fails to place an offering there, he believes the spirit may do some harm to him or to some member of his family.

Continuing to speak of spirits, the missionary told about an unusual wedding held in his church in Rangoon. The Burmese couple wanted their wedding to be like those held in the West. They had flower girls and ring bearers as well as bridesmaids and groomsmen. There was quite a number of persons in the bridal procession.

As the organ began to play the wedding march, the minister came out, followed by the groom and the best man. Then the other young men and young women began to come down the aisle. Coming before the bride were two flower girls and two ring bearers, all of them small children. Just in front of these was another little girl carrying a mirror.

The minister was surprised to see a mirror carried in a wedding procession. Of course he could not stop the little girl in the midst of the procession and ask why she had brought a mirror; but just as soon as the wedding was over, he went to a Burmese man, a member of the bride's family, and asked him. Flowers and rings belonged in a wedding, but why the mirror?

The explanation was this: the Burmese believe that spirits attend weddings. They might cause trouble if not driven away. Now although the members of this wedding party were Christians, they had not been Christians long enough to throw off all their fear of spirits. They needed more teaching and better understanding. In a Burmese wedding a mirror is carried before the bride to frighten off any evil spirit that might have come in. The idea is that if an evil spirit sees his face in a mirror he is so startled at the horrible sight of himself that he will run away in a hurry.

The missionary had many visits with the bride and groom after the wedding day, and he helped them to see that the Christian way of life is faith in God and we have no need to fear evil spirits.

The apostle James, in his letter, speaks of the use of a mirror. He says that too many people look into a mirror and then go away and forget what they look like. He probably meant that each one must really look at himself and see a deeper need than that which he can see in the looking glass. One's face might be clean and still his thoughts and his heart be unclean. So James says: "But he who looks into the perfect law, the law of liberty, and perseveres, being no hearer that forgets but a doer that acts, he shall be blessed in his doing."

You see, James thinks of the Bible as a perfect mirror. He is right too. As we read the Bible we can read about ourselves. We can see a picture of our own lives and learn just what God wants us to do and to be as his sons and daughters.

56

We need mirrors to use when we comb our hair and wash our faces. We need the mirror James refers to also. As you read your Bible, see if you can see yourself there. If you look closely and read carefully, you will see two images—the one that shows you what you are like now, and the one that shows what you could be if God had his way with your life.

* * *

13

HEAD-HUNTERS BECOME SOUL WINNERS

> Create in me a clean heart, O God, and put
> a new and right spirit within me.—PS. 51:10

WHAT ARE SOME of the greatest changes you can think about? Think hard. May I make some suggestions?

Close your eyes and think about the darkest night you ever knew. The moon is not shining. No stars are out, for the clouds are heavy in the sky. It is so black you feel you could cut the darkness with a knife.

Now open your eyes and look around you. The sun is shining. The sky is without a cloud. The day is bright and beautiful. This is a really big change from the darkness of night to sunshine.

Close your eyes again—tight. Now think of the coldest winter day you can remember. The temperature is below zero. The snow is deep. The wind is blowing a gale, and the sleet is cracking against the windowpanes like BB shot. This is really a terrible day.

Open your eyes and see that the winter cold and sleet are gone. It is springtime. The flowers are blooming and the birds are singing. It is a wonderful warm morning for all to enjoy.

There is a great change when the sun shines and drives away the darkness. There is a great change when the summer comes and the winter cold is gone. But the greatest changes are found—not in the out-of-doors, or in nature—but in the lives of people. The greatest change of all comes in the heart of a person when God is allowed to take over inside.

Close your eyes again. Close them very tight, for we are going to take a long journey. We will fly over the land, over the mountains, over the ocean, and land on the other side of the globe, in Assam. Up in the Naga hills in this wild country are wild men and women. They are dark-skinned and wear very little clothing. They paint their faces to make them frightful and carry long knives and spears. Do you know that these wild men of the Naga hills actually kill people and cut off their heads to offer as sacrifices to their idols? Horrible as it is, this is part of their heathen worship.

Now open your eyes wide, for I want to tell you a wonderful true story that shows the power of God to make the greatest of all changes in the hearts of men.

Many years ago some Christian missionaries went to

visit the head-hunters. Although they were told of the danger and were advised to carry guns with them, they did not take any weapons at all. Instead they took their Bibles, and one man took along his violin.

As this little group of missionaries walked along the jungle path, the way became narrower and narrower. The trees seemed higher and closer, and the branches and underbrush heavier and heavier. It was difficult to get through. Then suddenly, in front of them, on both sides of them, and behind them, the faces of savages popped up. These were angry faces, and soon hands came into view holding knives and spears.

The missionaries were frightened, but they trusted in God to take care of them. They believed he would. The man with the violin began to play a hymn—"My Faith Looks Up to Thee." The savages seemed to like the music. They listened and their scowls changed to smiles. They lowered their spears and knives.

When the missionary had finished the hymn, the savages made motions for more music. The missionary started another hymn and his friends sang as he played. Several hymns were played and sung, for the head-hunters wanted more and more. Finally the savages motioned for the missionaries to follow them. They wanted to take them to the village so that their wives and children could hear the music. There the missionaries sang more songs, and the savages smiled because they knew these visitors were friends.

After quite a long time, the missionaries let the savages know by their signs that they must go back to their own village but would come and sing for them again at another time. It took many visits before the missionaries were able to talk with the Nagas and explain about God and his love, but after some time they were able to make them understand. The men and women and boys and girls were delighted with the good news. After many visits over many months they became Christians.

Today, a wonderful change has taken place in that hill country. You can go there and find many Christian churches and many fine Christian people. They have their own ministers too, and their church leaders and they themselves are sending out missionaries to other tribes to tell them about God's love and the way of salvation.

The missionaries have hospitals in the Naga country and minister to the sick in the name of the Great Physician. One of the greatest changes to be found anywhere in the world is among the nurses in these hospitals. Do you know that some of the nurses who are ministering to sick patients in the name of Christ and helping to bring them back to health again are granddaughters of men who once were head-hunters? Think of the power of God's love that can change the hearts of men and women and make soul winners out of head-hunters. These former head-hunters no longer want to hurt or harm anyone. They wish only to be good neighbors and share their best as friends in Christ.

God is at work in nature, changing night into day, and winter into summer. But the most wonderful changes of God are those he makes within the hearts of men. Bad men are made into good men. Enemies are changed into friends. Wild savages become Christian brothers and sisters and take their places in the family circle of our heavenly Father.

FROM
NATURE

* * *

14

ACTING LIKE YEAST

> The kingdom of heaven is like leaven which
> a woman took and hid in three measures of
> meal, till it was all leavened.—MATT. 13:33

GRANDMOTHER and GRANDFATHER had come for a visit. Cathy and Becky were so excited they told all their friends, and all wanted to get a look at Grandmother and Grandfather. In fact the visiting grandparents were shared with all the children of the neighborhood.

The neighbors were very thoughtful and kind. Just as the family was sitting down at the supper table, there was a knock at the door. When the door was opened, in came the next-door neighbor bearing a wonderful big chocolate cake. It was a beautiful gift and greatly appreciated and enjoyed.

The next day Cathy said, "Grandmother, why don't

you and I make something and take it next door as Mrs. Curtis did for us last night!"

That was a fine idea, so Grandmother and Cathy got busy in the kitchen. Grandmother got out some large bowls and pans and Cathy got her small cooking pans, and the mixing and fixing began in earnest.

First, some milk was warmed and put in a bowl. Then salt, sugar, shortening, and a small bit of yeast were added.

Cathy said, "What is that you are putting in now, Grandmother?"

"That," said Grandmother, "is yeast, and I'll tell you a story about it. Once when Jesus was talking about his kingdom he said it is like yeast which a woman took and put in some meal she was mixing up. You see Jesus wanted to explain that although only a little yeast was put in, it soon spread over the entire lump of dough and made it rise so the bread would be light and good."

Then Grandmother added flour and mixed up the dough and showed Cathy how the lump got larger and must be worked down again and again until it was ready to put in the oven to bake. She explained that it was the little bit of yeast added to the flour that made the dough rise.

As they worked together, Grandmother told Cathy that they could make many kinds of bread and rolls out of that batch of dough. They added more sugar, some butter, cinnamon, and nuts and rolled out some of the dough into a flat piece. Then they rolled it together to make a delicious breakfast roll. They made other parts of

63

the dough into buns and pocket rolls, but the largest part they put into pans to bake into loaves of bread.

Cathy took some of each kind of dough and put it into her small pans and put them into the oven with the larger pans Grandmother used.

While the bread and rolls were cooking, Grandmother talked with Cathy about the yeast and the remark Jesus made about it.

"Good people," said Grandmother, "are like yeast because they give a lift to the whole neighborhood in which they live. Their lives help other people who live around them to understand something of God's purpose for them. The whole community is made better because the good people live there, even though they are few in number."

"Mrs. Curtis was like yeast when she brought that nice cake to our house last night," said Cathy.

"That is exactly right," said Grandmother.

"We will be acting like yeast when we take this loaf of bread and these rolls over to Mrs. Curtis' house, won't we, Grandmother?"

"Yes," said Grandmother, "and wouldn't it be wonderful if people could be such good neighbors all over our city, and all over our country, and all over our world?"

"That would be great, and it's fun too. You know, Grandmother, I like to act like yeast," said Cathy as she took her pan of rolls out of the oven and prepared to take them over next door to give to her neighbor's daughter Gale Elizabeth.

15

THE TINY SEED THAT SPLIT THE MIGHTY ROCK

> *The kingdom of heaven is like a grain of mustard seed.* —MATT. 13:31

JESUS USED MANY parables to help his hearers understand the gospel of the kingdom of God. One day he talked about seeds which a farmer sowed in his field. He spoke of good soil and bad soil and harvests. One of the most interesting of the seed parables referred to the small size of the seed and the great size of the shrub it produces.

Would you think that a small seed could split a rock? It sounds ridiculous to talk of a seed cracking a rock, but not only is it possible; it often happens.

If you have traveled in the woods a great deal and have kept your eyes open, you may have seen a great stone—perhaps as big as the room of a house—with a tree growing through the middle of it. You might wonder how such a thing could happen.

On a trail which young people used to travel frequently on their Sunday afternoon hikes, there were such a rock and such a tree. It was a pine tree and it stood like a giant, pushing two boulders aside as it rose upward toward the sky.

If you went up close and studied the rock and the tree,

you could see just what happened. Long, long ago a pine cone, or a scale from a cone, was blown by the wind and lodged in a crack on top of that great rock. This small scale or ovule is the seed of the pine tree. Like any good seed it is alive and ready to sprout and grow if given moisture and sunshine. When the summer shower wet the rock, the pine seed began to sprout. It sent down little rootlets that crept into the tiny crack in the rock. The rock soaked up water from the earth and nourished the little pine seed.

As the summer wore on, the tiny pine seedling grew, putting a branch upward toward the sky and sending more roots downward through the crack in the rock.

Life is always stronger than death, and the live pine was stronger than the dead rock. After many summers and many long winters it split the rock wide open. Finally the end of the roots reached the ground beneath the rock. Then, with more nourishment from the soil, it grew stronger and the trunk expanded. The branches reached out, and the growing tree pushed the rock aside as an athlete pushes great weights by flexing his strong muscles.

But Jesus was not interested in seeds in the same way a farmer is interested as he plants them in his field. Jesus was illustrating the power of the gospel he preached. He wanted his disciples to take his teachings and use them to live better lives. He did not tell them exactly what they should do day by day, but he gave them good ideas which, like seeds, would grow into good deeds and become good habits of life.

For instance, in Jesus' day there were many slaves in the land. People owned other people and made them work for them without wages. These slaves could be bought and sold just like horses and cows. Jesus did not tell his disciples, "You must free all the slaves and do away with this terrible practice." He wanted Christian people to see for themselves the great evil of such a system. So he planted a thought seed. Jesus said, "All men are brothers." Then as Christian men and women in the church began to think about this fact, they said, "Surely we cannot make slaves of our brothers!" So Christian men and women decided to do away with slavery.

The same thing was true of the treatment of little children. Long ago children were thought of as things rather than as people with minds and wills and souls of their own. Children were mistreated and often beaten and were sometimes even sold to pay off debts. But Christian fathers and mothers found the seed of a new idea in their hearts. Jesus said, "Let the children come to me, and do not hinder them; for to such belongs the kingdom of heaven." If children are important to Jesus, then they should be important to his followers. So Christian parents thought differently about their children and taught that all children everywhere should be loved and cared for.

And so it has been with all the important things in life. The gospel of Jesus plants idea and ideal seeds in the minds and hearts of men and women. These grow into new and better ways of solving problems and of living together. In this way, as seed ideas grow and life becomes more and more what Jesus planned for it to be, the Kingdom itself is being formed. That is at least part of what Jesus meant when he said, "The kingdom of heaven is like a grain of mustard seed."

* * *

16

HE LEADS ME

He leads me in paths of righteousness for his name's sake. —PS. 23:3

KING DAVID EXPRESSED in the twenty-third psalm his firm belief that God was always caring for him and always leading him in right paths. He had learned that lesson when he tended sheep as a boy. Just as a shepherd cares for his sheep and leads them in safe places, so God directs our lives.

When Jesus was teaching his disciples, he took them out into the fields and pointed to the birds and the flowers. He reminded them that God cares for all the creatures of the out-of-doors and provides for their needs. He taught them a lesson by contrast—"Are you not of more value than they?"

Wherever we look we may see illustrations of God's watch care in the world he has made. We are familiar

with the flight of birds southward in the fall and north-
ward in the spring. Did you ever hear of the migration
of fish? There are many kinds of fish that move in
"schools" and travel great distances. One of the most
unusual stories of migration is seen in the life story of
the Chinook salmon.

We all know something about the salmon, for we have
seen it canned for table use and have eaten its pink meat.
Let us go to the Far West and follow a salmon from
the time it is born into the world until—well, until it
arrives in the can!

Salmon come from pink-colored eggs about the size
of a small pea. The "nests" of eggs are found in the
small streams that flow into the rivers that finally empty
into the Pacific Ocean along the coast of Washington
and Oregon. The young salmon minnow is silvery in
appearance and very small at first, but when he is a year
old he is about five inches long and looks like the full-
grown fish that are fifteen or twenty inches long and
weigh several pounds.

About this time this "young fry" salmon begins working his way down the stream toward the river. He does
not swim constantly downstream but plays around in
one pool after another and pauses here and there to pick
up bugs and flies and the many water nymphs that make
up his food. He must be careful about enemies too.
Wild ducks and herons, as well as kingfishers and fish
hawks, like to eat young salmon, and they can catch them
if the fish are not quick in darting beyond their reach.
Mink and raccoons also are good fishermen and catch

many of the young salmon as they move along near the banks of the stream.

After several months the salmon reaches the ocean. Here quite a change occurs, for he has been swimming in fresh water, and the water of the ocean is salty. To accustom himself to the different kind of water, the young salmon stays some time in the mouth of the river, where the fresh water mixes with the salt water. He will swim out into the ocean for a little while and then back into the fresh water until he finds he can remain in the salt water. He prefers the salt water because there is so much food in the sea. He finds whole schools of small shrimp and other small sea fish that he likes to eat. In fact, he is able to eat so much of his favorite food that he soon grows in size and becomes a large fish.

The salmon lives in the ocean water for three or four years and probably travels several hundred miles up and down the coast and out into the depths of the sea. Then an unusual thing happens. The salmon, together with all the other salmon in his school, begins to feel an urge to go back to fresh water and to swim against the current up the rivers that empty into the ocean.

The most amazing fact in this part of the salmon story is that each salmon seems to want to find the exact stream where he was born, and by some strange instinct he is able to locate that very stream. You see, this is made more difficult by the fact that so many little streams branch off from the main river that flows into the ocean. First, the salmon must swim up the right river—the Columbia, for instance. Then he must swim up and up the stream until he comes to the right branch, then up that branch to a smaller stream that branches off, until he finally reaches the small creek where he was born.

Several other difficulties face the salmon as he tries to get back to the little stream where he was born. He encounters many waterfalls and dams and must jump over the rapids and falls to continue up the river. Sometimes he must jump great heights to get over the waterfall. The government has arranged fish "ladders" at the sites of the big dams. By use of the ladder the salmon can climb up from the lower level to the higher level by jumping a step at a time into pools formed by small dams arranged in the form of a water stairway.

Then there are other hazards facing the salmon. Fishermen are trying to catch him with hooks and lines. Others have permission to catch him with traps and nets for the canneries. Wild animals are also on the lookout for the migrating salmon and lie in wait for him near the shallow pools in the small streams higher up in the hills. Bears can catch salmon in these areas; and raccoons, mink, and otter also catch quite a number.

So, of the many schools of salmon that start up the river toward the small streams where they were born, and where they themselves will lay eggs to hatch other baby salmon, few actually complete their journey. The ones that do, make "nests" by brushing the rocks in the bottom of the stream into a hollow bowl-like depression. There they lay their eggs. Then the salmon soon die, and their bodies float down the stream or are eaten by birds or animals.

Men who have studied the habits of the salmon have wondered about their strange ability to find their way back to the exact stream and place where they began life as tiny minnows. Perhaps you and I can answer this question as well as the most learned scientist. The salmon are directed by the same God of whom King David said, "He leads me."

* * *

17

LIKE A TREE

> *He is like a tree planted by streams of water,*
> *that yields its fruit in its season, and its leaf*
> *does not wither. In all that he does, he prospers.*
> —PS. 1:3

THE WRITER OF THE first psalm thinks of a good man as being like a tree. He speaks of the leaves that do not dry up and the fruit which is produced year after year.

When one learns a great deal about trees, he sees why the psalmist compared the good man to a tree.

Trees are the largest plants in the world. They are not like bushes or vines. They stand up higher than houses and are permanent. They do not grow up in the springtime and die down in the fall. The leaves fall off, but the tree, like a tall giant, stands through storm and sunshine, through winter and summer.

There are many kinds of trees, but they can be divided generally into two classes. Some shed their leaves, and some are evergreens. Those that shed their leaves are called the "broadleaf" trees, and the evergreens are the "needle-leaf" trees. The broadleaf trees are also called the hardwoods, and the needle-leaf trees, the softwoods, though some of the evergreens have harder wood than some of the leaf-shedding trees.

Trees are found all over the world. There are more than a thousand different varieties. They give shade and beauty to people and furnish wood, fruit, and nuts.

In fact, trees are so "friendly" and people have enjoyed being near trees so much they are often thought of as persons. Poets write about trees in this way, and many people refer to them in endearing terms.

There are many famous trees, such as the Cambridge Elm in Cambridge, Massachusetts, under which George Washington took command of the Continental Army in 1775. The Charter Oak in Hartford, Connecticut, got its name from the fact that the charter of the state was hidden in this tree to protect it from enemies in 1687. The General Sherman tree, in the Sequoia National Park in California, is claimed to be the largest and oldest living thing in the world.

Most of us have our favorite tree or trees. We may choose a favorite tree because of its beauty, such as a dogwood, a magnolia, or a catalpa; or because of its fine fruit, such as an apple, a cherry, or a pear tree; or because we like to climb it or have a tree house built in its branches. Trees are often used as meeting places, and many picnics are held under their spreading branches.

A tree might be likened to a factory. It is constantly at work, drawing up water, circulating, manufacturing, and delivering. The roots are a very important part of this process even though we cannot see them. The main roots branch off into smaller roots, and the smaller ones into still smaller branches, and at the end are the tiny "hair" roots. These tiny white hair roots collect the moisture from the soil. It is then drawn up through the roots to the trunk. There are "pipe lines" that run up the trunk of the tree and out the branches to the leaves. It is said that a large apple tree will lift as much as ninety-six gallons of water in one day's time. When you think of the distance from the ground to the top of the tree and to the tips of the branches, you realize this is quite an accomplishment.

The sap, or water with minerals from the ground, goes up from the roots, through the trunk, to the upper branches and leaves. The leaves, with the help of sunlight, manufacture food for the tree. This food is then sent back down other pipe lines to feed the trunk and the roots.

We have described a "good" tree, but not all trees are good. A good tree is one which is strong and healthy and bears good fruit. Some trees are unhealthy. They bear no fruit, or produce fruit that is sour or wormy and therefore useless.

Sometimes during a windstorm a big tree will topple

over. When this happens it is usually because the tree was rotten inside. Although the outer bark looked healthy and firm, the inside wood was eaten away by insects or was dead and decaying.

Jesus, you will remember, once condemned a fig tree because it was flying false colors. By its leaves it announced that it was bearing fruit. The fruit and the leaves come at the same time on the fig tree. Since it was pretending to be what it was not, Jesus said, "May no fruit ever come from you again!"

A good man is like a good tree because he is strong, he is steady and dependable, and he is constantly at work. The result of his work, like the fruit of a tree, is helpful to others. All this is possible because of God's gifts both to the tree and to the man.

As you look at a graceful, friendly fruit tree, and then look at yourself, do you find that you too are like a tree?

* * *

18

MR. AND MRS. HIGH HOLE

> The trees of the Lord are watered abundantly,
> the cedars of Lebanon which he planted.
> In them the birds build their nests.
> —PS. 104:16-17

WALKING THROUGH THE woods recently I met an old friend. Evidently he had been living in his new

75

apartment for some time, but I had not seen him before. He flew in just as I was going by. You see, my friend is a flicker, or yellowhammer. He is the large brown and yellow woodpecker known so well all over the country for his friendliness and his interesting ways.

I'm sure you have met Mr. Flicker. You may not have known him by name, but you must have seen him. He is a large bird, larger than a robin, but smaller than a pigeon. Sometimes he is mistaken for a meadow lark because he likes to feed on the ground, in the field or on the lawn, and is often seen with other birds. He is a friendly bird and gets along well with his bird neighbors and is not always quarreling with them, or pecking at them, as is the habit of some other birds.

Flickers usually build their nests in a tree by hollowing out a hole high up from the ground. For this reason they are often called "High Holes." For their purpose they usually pick a tree with dead wood, which is easier to cut into. When the nest is ready the female flicker lays five to eight eggs.

Right here we might pause to say that the flicker is a determined bird and does not easily get discouraged or give up. A naturalist who wanted to test the determination of a flicker took one egg out of her nest when only two were laid. The flicker laid another egg next day, and the naturalist took that away too. Amazing as it may seem, day after day an egg was laid by the flicker, and just as regularly the egg was removed by the man. It was recorded that in seventy-three days that flicker laid seventy-one eggs. You might say that bird really believed in the motto, "If at first you do not succeed, try, try again!"

Flickers like to make a lot of noise. When I was a boy, we lived next door to the church. This was a large structure and the high gables were finished off at the top with sheet-iron blocks that looked like capstones. A boy with a twenty-two rifle had shot holes in one of these sheet-iron "capstones." One spring I remember being awakened about sunrise morning after morning by a loud r-r-r-r-r- just outside my window. When I looked out I saw a yellowhammer, or flicker, drumming away at that sheet iron. I used to laugh at the flicker, because I supposed he thought the holes were made by another woodpecker and he wanted to prove that his beak was as tough as that of the first fellow who punctured the metal. Later, however, when I studied about flickers, I found that all male flickers like to drum on tin or sheet iron such as that found in eaves troughs. They make this loud drumming sound to attract their mates. It sound like just a lot of noise to us, but it must sound like music to the female flickers. At any rate, it attracts their attention and helps the birds get on with their love-making.

Some birds are considered harmful by farmers because they eat their seed before it can sprout and grow, or they eat the grain before the farmer can harvest it. Some of them also eat berries and spoil fruit by feeding on it as it hangs on the trees. But the flicker is considered a helpful bird. He feeds mainly on insects, particularly ants.

77

One flicker was found to have five thousand ants in his stomach.

When I saw that flicker in the tree nest in the woods, I thought of the words of the psalmist:

> The trees of the Lord are watered abundantly,
>   the cedars of Lebanon which he planted.
> In them the birds build their nests.

There are many kinds of birds' nests. Eagles pile up large bundles of sticks and build nests high up in lone pine trees which can be seen for great distances. Some birds, like the weaverbird and the oriole, actually weave a kind of bag for their nests. Swallows plaster mud on the walls of barns, and bank swallows dig holes in the sides of cliffs. But it is God who "watered abundantly the cedars" and he also planted them and made them grow. God not only provides a place for the bird to build his nest, but also provides his food day by day, creates the life of the young birds in the eggs, and cares for them and all the creatures that live in this, our Father's World.

19

BUSY AS A BEAVER

> . . . always abounding in the work of the Lord.
> —I COR. 15:58

IF ANYONE WHO knows you well reports that you are "busy as a beaver," take it as a very fine compliment, for surely it is meant to be one.

Although you may not have seen beavers, you certainly have heard about them. They are both interesting and useful, and that is why I want to tell you the story of Bobby Beaver.

Bobby, and each of his family for that matter, looks very much like a big fat squirrel, with a few differences. Of course he isn't a squirrel, and he doesn't have a bushy tail. His tail is flat like a canoe paddle. He doesn't eat nuts either. In fact, he would not care for nuts, even for dessert. His food is bark from trees, especially aspen trees, the roots of water plants, and twigs. For dessert he likes the tender stems of water lilies. Like all beavers he lives in streams or lakes, for beavers are water animals.

Bobby is a good swimmer. Instead of having to put rubber fins on his feet to give him speed in the water, he actually has fins of skin between the toes of his hind feet. He likes to dive and to swim under water. He must swim under water to enter his house, for the door is down deep in the lake or stream where he lives.

Bobby's house is an interesting one, and Bobby built it himself. He is an architect and also an engineer. I will speak of his engineering skill later, but just now let's examine his house, or "lodge." This is built of sticks, rocks, and mud. It has two floors and two rooms, one on each floor. The upper room is the living room, where Bobby stays most of the time when he is home with his family. It is dry and warm. The lower room is his store-room, in which he keeps his food supply of bark, twigs, and roots. To enter his house, Bobby must dive deep in the water and come in at the tunnel opening into a long hallway that leads to his storehouse. His living room has an opening for air in the top, and this is carefully concealed with many twigs and dead leaves.

Bobby is also an engineer and he works quite a bit on this kind of business. You see it is necessary in the colony where Bobby and his beaver friends live to have plenty of water. In order to keep the water level high all the year around, dams must be built to hold the water back. Bobby and all the beavers in the colony, both old and young, work on the dam. They cut down trees—or, more accurately, they gnaw down trees. To fell a tree, a beaver, standing on his hind legs and bracing himself with his flat tail, begins gnawing off the bark of a tree all the way around. Then he gnaws into the wood and keeps working until the tree falls. Several beavers will get busy gnawing off all the boughs and branches until just a log is left. They cut this log up into lengths they can float or drag to the place where they are making the dam.

The beavers always do this work at night, and they like best to work by the light of a full moon. They find a narrow place with a rock bottom in the stream, or a projecting rock or tree where they can anchor their dam and give it a solid base. Then they place the logs and branches across the stream, weaving them together so they will stay in place, and add rocks to hold it steady. They get mud, carrying it with their forepaws against their breasts, and plaster the dam so that it becomes like masonry. When the dam is finished, it may not look very artistic, but it will hold back the water, and very soon the beavers have a fine pond. Here they build their houses and live happily with their families.

Since many trees are needed by the beavers for food and for making their dams and houses, the trees nearby will, in time, be all used up. So the beavers dig canals out from their ponds to reach other trees which they can cut down and float to the pond and to their storehouses.

Bobby and his family have a long and honorable record. They do not cause trouble with other animals or get into fights with one another—that is, not often. They are peaceful animals and their way of life is helpful to their human neighbors too. Their dams hold back the water and prevent floods. Their ponds are good wildlife spots where fish can live and waterfowl build their nests.

It is said that Bobby's family helped to build America. Many of Bobby's forefathers gave their lives for this country. Their flesh was eaten as food and kept many people from starving, and their hides were sold to make fur garments. In the early days in America when money was very scarce, beaver hides were used in many places for money. Instead of figuring in money the price of a house, a cow, a canoe, or a gun, the people would say, "This is worth ten beaver hides," or twenty or thirty, as the case might be.

Bobby and his friends are still helping America grow today. Often beavers are trapped by conservation men and taken to other parts of the country where they are needed to build their dams so that ponds will be made and wildlife will have plenty of water for their needs.

Bobby Beaver is a good animal friend to know. He works hard; he gets along well with his family and neighbors; and his work is the kind that helps build a better place for all to enjoy.

FROM THE
JUNIOR CLASS

* * *

20

MINUTE BOYS

> *. . . to be ready for any honest work.*
> —TIT. 3:1

THE BOYS of the junior department felt left out of the larger program of the church. They enjoyed their church school sessions, and they always attended the first part of the worship service, remaining until the juniors went to their own departmental rooms for the extended session. But they wanted to take part in the "big" church program too.

As they talked things over, Jim said, "Fellows, we are considered too young to be junior deacons or junior trustees. We are asked to usher on Children's Day and on Youth Sunday, but that is about the only chance we get."

"There must be some place we can be used," said

John. "If there isn't a place now, I am in favor of making a place."

That idea seemed to please the whole group, but no one had a suggestion as to where they could fit in. So they decided to think it over and have another get-together the next Sunday morning.

Ideas have a way of popping up almost anywhere and any time. Sometimes they hit a person at a very unexpected moment. Wallace was sitting at the dinner table on Thursday evening when an idea hit him like the wallop of a bumblebee.

"I've got it!" he shouted and jumped up from his chair.

"What on earth is the matter with you, Wallace?" asked his mother. "You act like you have been sparked by an electric current!"

"That's just about what happened," answered Wallace. "I have an idea for our junior department boys. You know, I talked to you about our plan. We want to do something for the church, but no one knew just what to suggest. Now I have something really good to tell the fellows!"

Wallace thought the idea was so good it would not wait until Sunday. His mother was very glad to do her part to speed things along and suggested that the boys all come over to the house after school next day. They could have a talkfest while they refreshed themselves with cookies and lemonade.

So next afternoon the whole gang was there, and all were eager to know about the plan Wallace had in mind.

"Don't keep us waiting," urged Don. "Tell us about the big idea, Wallace."

"Well, it may not be so big," said Wallace, "but I do think it may be one you will like. You know, in our history class last fall we studied about the minutemen. They were the New England farmers who trained to be soldiers just before the Revolutionary War. You remember they kept their guns by them while they plowed. Whenever they were needed they would go 'at a minute's notice'."

"My suggestion is this. There are a lot of times when things are needed at the church and someone must be called on 'at a moment's notice.' There are errands that must be run and other things needing to be done at the last minute. Why don't our junior department boys organize as 'minute boys'? Whenever the pastor, a deacon, or one of the church school teachers needs an errand run in a hurry or wants someone on the spur of the moment to help, all they need to do is summon a minute boy for the job."

Minute boys! That struck the whole group with a bang. Minute boys they wanted to be, and minute boys they would plan to be, for ever-ready service to the church.

Even though you have an idea, it takes a lot of thinking and planning to work out the details and get it going. The junior boys got their heads together and threw in all the ideas they could think of that Friday afternoon. When Sunday came they were all at the church early and each one had a few more ideas to contribute.

85

They called on their teachers—Mr. Seelye, Mr. Acker, and Mr. Whitenack—to help them. Together they organized their program, and soon they had a service offer to make to the pastor.

The pastor was delighted to meet the boys. He said he thought their plan was a splendid one. Often, he said, there had been times when he had needed to call an usher or a deacon to make a trip for him at the last minute. He said he would much rather have had a minute boy than one of these older men. Minute boys would be much quicker and much easier to locate.

So the plan was started on the first Sunday of the month, and every boy was eager to have a job to do. Not all of them were called on at once. From time to time, however, different ones had their opportunity. The pastor had told them in the beginning, "Service is not just doing, but also being ready to be used when needed."

The boys adopted a badge to identify them as minute boys—a circle, like the face of a watch, with just a minute hand pointing to one minute to twelve. They also kept small notebooks to record their errands so that they could remember them and report at meetings later. It took patience to be a minute boy, as well as willingness to run when called upon. But these boys tried to carry out their motto, *Ready to Serve*.

21

THANKS FOR EVERYTHING!

Always and for everything giving thanks in the name of our Lord Jesus Christ to God the Father.   —EPH. 5:20

THE SUPERINTENDENTS of the church school paid a visit to the junior department. There are two superintendents, for both Mr. and Mrs. Snyder are superintendents. They are called "cosuperintendents." Many of the classes also have coteachers—husbands and wives teaching the class together.

When Mr. and Mrs. Snyder came into the junior department on this particular Sunday morning, all the boys and girls knew it was a special visit. It was not just a "look in" to see how things were going. A request was to be made of the juniors.

Mr. Snyder explained the idea. "We have been talking with the pastor and we believe you juniors can help us to have a better worship service on Sunday morning. Of course, you boys and girls are always present at the worship service, and you help in the singing and the praying of the Lord's prayer and the responsive reading. But we want you, once in a while at least, to take a leading part in the service."

"Do you really think the juniors could take a part by

87

themselves in the 'big service'?" asked the junior department superintendent.

Miss Scott knew, of course, that the juniors could make a real contribution to the worship program in the sanctuary, but she wanted to hear Mr. Snyder say he was sure they could. And this is exactly what he did say.

"I not only think they can make a contribution," said Mr. Snyder, "but I know it will be helpful to everyone there. Now here is what I want you to do on Sunday morning, three weeks from today. I think this will give you plenty of time to prepare, and your part will be printed on the order of service for that day.

"I want you to write your own litany of thanks. Every service should have a litany or prayer of thanks as well as one of confession and dedication. I want you to think of the many things you are thankful for, write them down, and work out a litany.

"Now, this is what I mean by a litany. Part of you will make statements; and the rest of you, or all together, will give answers. For instance, one group will say, *'For sending us Jesus to be our teacher and saviour.'* Then all will answer, *'We give thanks, O Lord.'* We want you to work out your own litany instead of copying it from a hymnal. You may look in the back of the hymnal for some samples, but write your own. I know you can do it, and Mrs. Snyder and I will be there to see and hear you."

That was a challenge, and the juniors were glad to take it. Some time was saved after the class session to do some talking about the litany. The whole department worked together. First, they thought of the different things for which they were thankful and which they wanted to include in their litany.

Wallace was good at printing, so he was asked to go to the board and write down the different suggestions as they were made.

"All right now," said Miss Scott, "let's have some ideas. What are you thankful for?"

Ideas came thick and fast.

"I'm thankful for this church school," said Jim.

"And for our teachers," said Susan, "for it wouldn't be a church school without them."

"I'm thankful for the church itself," said Tom. "We wouldn't have a church school if it were not for the church."

So it went on and on. Mothers and fathers, sisters and brothers, were added to the list. Houses were also added and clothing and food, for all of these are important. Pets were mentioned, for they add to the fun of living. School was put in the list, of course, though some of the boys said they could get along without the "workhouse." They really did not mean such a thing, however; they knew how important schools are if boys and girls are to grow up to be understanding and able to take their places of leadership in the world.

Finally the board was filled with things to be thankful for, and the time was up. So a big sign was written in the corner of the board: Please Do Not Erase. It was decided to begin next Sunday to work the ideas into a litany to be used in the worship service.

Next Sunday every member of the junior department was present—right on time—because the program was a crowded one. First, there was the departmental worship, then the lesson period, and then the preparation of the litany.

It took lots of time to write the litany, and the wording was changed over and over before it was finally completed. Copy after copy was made. A word was erased here and one added there, until it was just the way everyone wanted it. Here is the litany the boys and girls of the junior department prepared and used in the worship service of their church:

> For the warmth of clothing
> *We thank thee, God.*
> For the food that makes us grow
> *We thank thee, God.*
> For our shelter that brings us happiness
> *We thank thee, God.*
> For our parents who tell us right from wrong
> *We thank thee, God.*
> For our churches and schools
> *We thank thee, God.*
> All: *Thank you, God, for everything!*

22

YOU WERE THERE!

> And the crowds that went before him and
> that followed him shouted, "Hosanna to the
> Son of David! Blessed be he who comes in the
> name of the Lord! Hosanna in the highest!"
> —MATT. 21:9

DON COULDN'T wait until the family got home to tell them about the exciting time his class had had at the church school session.

Mother said, "Don, it will surely keep. Wait until dinner time, and all of us can listen at the table."

"But, Mother, this is something different—you don't understand," said Don. "Did you ever crawl inside a donkey?" he added, trying to stir up some curiosity.

"Crawl inside a donkey! Whoever heard such a foolish idea!" said his mother.

"Well, that is just what Ward did this morning, and I was a mind reader myself," Don continued.

That was enough to make every member of the family eager to hear about what had happened in the junior department that Sunday morning. When dinner was on the table and Daddy had returned thanks, Mother turned to Don and said, "All right, Don, now we are ready to

91

hear all about the unusual things that happened in your class this morning."

"I'm not sure I can tell it so you will feel like all of us kids in the junior department felt, but I'll try," began Don. "You see it all had to do with Mrs. Howell's idea of having us do some thinking for ourselves and try to live the Bible stories rather than just listen to them.

"I'll try to remember the words Mrs. Howell used. She asked us if we had ever got *inside* a picture frame. She meant that we usually just look at a picture from a distance. She wanted us to try to get right in there and be part of the picture ourselves.

"Then she showed us a picture that all of us had seen many times, but—I want to tell you—that picture will look different to us now whenever we see it. I guess we hadn't really seen it before."

"What picture are you talking about, Don?" broke in his mother.

"I'm sorry, Mother," said Don. "I could see that picture so clearly I thought all of you could see it too! It was the picture of Jesus riding into Jerusalem on Palm Sunday. I'm sure you remember it. Jesus is on a young donkey. The disciple John is leading the donkey. Three small children are running along in front carrying flowers. Crowds of people are watching from both sides of the road. They are waving palm branches and singing. One woman is laying a beautiful rug down for the donkey to walk over. All the people seem to be very happy. Their faces are bright and they are smiling at Jesus."

92

"But what about this 'crawling inside a donkey'?" said sister Ann.

"I was just getting to that part," said Don. "You see if you walk back of the frame and really get into a picture, you must be one of the persons or animals in the picture. Mrs. Howell asked each of us to look at the picture very closely, decide which character we wanted to be, and then imagine just what we would think and say if we actually were there.

"Now, about 'crawling inside a donkey,' Ward likes ponies and dogs and all kinds of animals. He has a pony, as you know. So he wanted to try to think what it was like to be the donkey Jesus rode on that great day. He thought a long time, and this is what he wrote to read to the rest of us: 'No one ever rode on me before, but this man can ride me any time. He is the kindest person I ever saw. He did not kick me or scold me or yell at me. He just patted my head and rubbed my ears. He got on my back so gently I did not mind at all. I am proud to be in this procession, carrying this great man, with everyone singing and praising him.' "

"Who did you try to be, Don?" asked Ann.

"I tried to be John the beloved disciple," said Don. "In the picture he is leading the donkey and he is looking at Jesus just as you would expect the beloved disciple to look. I think he was saying to himself: 'Jesus is the most wonderful man I have ever known. He is more than a man. He is the Christ. He is God's own Son. He is my Saviour and my Lord. I love him. I shall love him—always!'

"I don't remember all the things that the fellows and girls said," continued Don, "but different ones tried to think like different people in the picture. I want to tell you one thing for sure, that picture really came alive! Whenever I look at it again, I will think I can hear the different people talking to me, and I know I shall hear all the crowd shouting and singing, 'Hosanna to the Son of David! Blessed be he who comes in the name of the Lord!' "

* * *

23

PUSH-BUTTON FACTORY

What is man that thou art mindful of him?

Thou hast made him little less than God.
—PS. 8:4-5

THE THIRD-YEAR juniors were all excited. Plans were made for the whole class to visit an automobile factory and actually see men building a car. Mr. Seelye, their teacher, said they would be able to watch a car being put together right from the start to the completed job.

So it was that on Saturday morning, bright and early, every member of the class was at the church, where two station wagons were waiting to take them to the automobile factory. When they arrived at the factory, each boy and girl signed the register. They were given safety glasses and told they must wear the glasses while in the factory buildings to protect their eyes.

At exactly nine o'clock all boarded a bus and were taken down the street and into the gate of the factory. There they went inside an open door and found an electric sight-seeing train waiting for them. There were three small cars with three double seats each and enough room for all the boys and girls to ride together. As they started down the aisle between great machines, all of which were running at high speed and making a din, they heard the voice of the guide and saw that each car had a loudspeaker on the dashboard so that everyone could hear.

The guide said that the interesting thing to watch was the automatic machinery. First they passed by the motor production line. Here were blocks of steel being carried along on a moving platform, and each time the line of motor blocks stopped for a brief second or two, a big machine came down and drilled a dozen or more holes, all at the same time. The guide said this multiple drill, which worked like automatic arms and fingers, performed twenty-six operations in one action! As the children rode along, they watched the engine, which began as just a block of metal, grow to look more and more complicated, and at the end of the line completed motors were "rolling off the assembly."

Then the electric train took the children past the mammoth presses. These were so tall it was necessary to look almost straight upward to see the top. They were also big and broad. Men were feeding large sheets of thin metal into these presses. Then the powerful machine came down and instantly the metal was formed into a fender. The children were told that to protect the men working on these giant machines, it was necessary to press two buttons before the press would work. In this way each man checked on his partner.

The operation that caused all the boys and girls to watch for several minutes was the automatic tire-mounting machine. Down the moving channel came automobile tires. When a tire came to a certain spot along the route, it was caused to flop over and fall on top of a metal wheel or rim. Then this loose tire and rim were moved under a press machine. Suddenly two arms came out and pressed the tire on the rim, and an air pressure machine inflated it with forty pounds of air, all in one operation. Some of the boys wanted to stay and watch this tire machine. They said they had helped their dads change tires, and it took a long time to do it by hand. This automatic machine did it in just about two seconds.

The most thrilling sight of all was the assembly line for the car itself. As the children watched, they saw an automobile chassis, or frame, swung onto a moving "chain" by a derrick. Then, as the frame moved along, men standing by attached the gas tank, the steering column, and the wheels. And even while the boys and girls were looking, the frame without stopping at all—began to look more and more like an automobile.

Suddenly there was a loud swishing sound, and a car body swooped down from the second floor and landed on the car frame. In a matter of seconds two men had fastened the body to the frame, and the car kept moving on to the end of the line.

Of course everything happened so rapidly that it is impossible to tell it all, but while the boys and girls looked, a complete car was made right before their eyes. A man climbed in and drove it off to test it before sending it away to be sold. The children saw the engine, the lights, and the brakes tested, and the finished car moved off to another "endless chain" that carried it down the aisle to the place where it was to be driven out of the factory.

You can imagine the kind of lesson that class had the next day when they came to the church school. Each one told what he remembered as being most interesting on the tour of the automobile factory. Practically everything was covered in their reports.

The teacher asked, "What was the most important thing in this whole push-button factory?"

That was a rather hard question to answer, because there were so many things that seemed very important. After a long discussion, however, all agreed that the men themselves were most important. Men made the wonder machines; men operated them; men supplied the power, the steel, and all the materials needed to make an automobile.

But, of course, when the class talked of the men, they remembered that God made them. So the class

97

that day came to a new understanding of the words of
the psalmist when he said:

> When I look at thy heavens, the work of thy fingers,
> the moon and the stars which thou hast established;
> what is man that thou art mindful of him,
> and the son of man that thou dost care for him?
> Yet thou hast made him little less than God,
> and dost crown him with glory and honor.

* * *

24

INDOOR SUNSHINE

I was sick and you visited me.—MATT. 25:36

AFTER THE PASTOR had preached on "Every
Member a Minister," the boys and girls in the junior department had a long session to talk about their part in
ministering for the church. What could boys and girls
do to help the pastor and the church?

They invited the pastor to come to their department
and talk with them about the things that were needed.
They wanted to have a list to choose from. The pastor
was glad to come to the junior department and was
pleased that the boys and girls were eager to serve in
the church program. He said their invitation was the

very first that had come to him. He had hoped that all the departments of the church school would offer their services, and they probably would, but the juniors were the first.

Several projects were listed by the pastor, such as arranging the hymnbooks in the racks each Saturday so they would be in order on Sunday morning, handing out leaflets at the door as the people came to the services, collecting the attendance cards left on the pews after the morning church service, and making posters announcing special church meetings and programs. The suggestion that pleased the children most was that they visit the shut-ins and cheer them up. The pastor said there was a large number of these members who were unable to come to the church but were very interested. He said the boys and girls would be most welcome as callers. They could probably make the shut-ins happier than could anyone else in the church, and the folk who were compelled to stay at home would be delighted if they knew the children were coming to see them.

So the juniors got their heads together to decide just how they would make the visits. They could sing for the people they visited, but they wanted to do much more. They thought of taking flowers, but flowers cost so much, and they did not have much money. They also thought of beautiful cards, but these too cost a great deal.

When Gladys went home from church school that day, she was thinking about these shut-ins and the flowers the juniors wanted to take them. Suddenly an idea came to her.

"Mother," she said, "you have just dozens of African violets. Why can't you let us have some of them to take with us when we go calling?"

"But would that really be a gift from you juniors?" asked Gladys' mother. "Wouldn't it be better for you to take something you yourselves had made or bought?"

"But we don't have enough money!" said Gladys.

"I'll tell you what you can do," said Mother. "African violets are very easy to grow. All you do is take a leaf from a plant and leave it in a glass of water until it starts to root. Then you put it in some dirt. You boys and girls can raise your own African violets and have plenty to take with you when you call."

Of course, that meant they could not go calling at once with violets as gifts. So the children decided to do several things. They would not delay their calls, but the first time they called they would sing for the shut-ins. It was during the Christmas season, and everyone likes to hear carols. They would also talk about the many interesting things going on at the church and give a sort of report on the church program.

Then the boys suggested that Christmas cards be taken too. They decided to make their own cards. What a busy and happy time they had at the church when they gathered to cut out pictures and paste together attractive greeting cards!

The calling began in December. It was loads of fun. There were so many calls to make that several days were set aside as calling days. On Sunday afternoon they made their first calls—on Mrs. Brown; Mr. Douglas; Mr. and

Mrs. Green; and a paralyzed boy, Tom Rolph, who was confined to a wheel chair. As they came to the house they would sing, "Joy to the World." Then, when the door was opened, they would all shout together, "Happy Holiday!" What a good-natured and happy crowd they were and what welcome visitors! It was hard to tell who had the most fun—the girls and boys, or the shut-ins they visited.

After the first calls were all made, the juniors had another planning session. They asked the girls to take care of planting African violets. The boys would find small pots for the plants, and both boys and girls would make the greeting cards. These cards were to be even more attractive than those bought in the stores, for they would be made especially for each person visited. They would also have something on them from the church—probably clipped from the weekly calendar or order of service. They all would have a lovely colored picture pasted on the front.

The visiting project of the juniors was one of the finest programs of the whole church. Everyone was talking of the good cheer and happiness the children scattered everywhere they went. With their songs, their flowers, and their greetings, they had gone out in the spirit of the Master, who said, "I was sick and you visited me."

25

THE HAPPY HUSTLERS

If ye know these things, happy are ye if ye do them.
—JOHN 13:17 (K.J.V.)

JIM AND HARRY had been having a wonderful week end together. Although they were cousins, this was the second visit together they had enjoyed in their whole lives. You see, Jim lived in Michigan, and Harry's home was out in California. This year was a very special year, and the whole family had planned to vacation together because Grandfather and Grandmother were celebrating their fortieth wedding anniversary. Of course, there were many cousins and the house was full and overflowing, but Jim and Harry were a bit special for each other because they were exactly the same age and had quite a lot in common, including stamp collections, rock and mineral samples, and model airplanes.

On Sunday Jim took Harry with him to Sunday school. Jim was proud of his church and liked to show his friends the beautiful Children's Center dedicated to the exclusive use of the boys and girls. He was especially proud of his Sunday school class. It was the third-year juniors, a class which could be found in any Sunday school anywhere in the country, but this third-year junior class was different. Its very name suggested a difference. Usually junior classes are referred to by number, or by their teacher, rather than by name.

Jim's class was called the "Happy Hustlers." If you saw them on Sunday morning, you would certainly get an idea of the meaning of the name. In the first place, every member would be present unless he was ill or away from town, and the class was a regular beehive of activity. It actually hummed on Sunday morning.

Jim was happy to introduce his cousin Harry to his teacher and to his fellow Happy Hustlers. Harry enjoyed every minute of the class period. Part of the time was given to reports of projects. This was new to Harry, and he listened intently as one after another of the boys and girls in the class reported on their many helpful acts during the past week—at home, at school, or on the playground. It seemed that they were constantly on the lookout for opportunities to be useful, and the variety of the activities reported proved that these boys and girls had a lot of imagination and were able to see chances that often are overlooked.

For instance, Mary had read the entire church bulletin to a member of the church who is blind. Mary said that she had been doing this for several weeks. Usually she would go over to Miss Jones's house after school to read to her, but this week she read the bulletin over the phone. Miss Jones listened to every word and thanked her over and over.

John reported on his weekly visit to a shut-in, Mr. Broadbeck. Mr. Broadbeck seemed to enjoy hearing all about the family night dinner at the church and asked if certain special friends of his were present. John knew most of these friends and was glad to be able to answer Mr. Broadbeck's questions.

Bill had been called by the church secretary and asked to drop by Mrs. Waterbury's house and leave her a copy of the "Secret Place" booklet, and he was glad to do this on his way to school.

The only trouble with that class session was the lack of time. Everything was so interesting and the time so short, that all of the reports could not be finished this week. Some were held over until next Sunday. The lesson was interesting too, for it was about Jesus feeding the five thousand people with the help of a junior boy who offered his lunch to Jesus.

When Harry and Jim were going home after church. Harry was telling how much he enjoyed the Sunday school class. He said, "Jim, that is an unusual class and it has an unusual name. Where did you get such a name anyhow?"

This was just the lead question Jim was waiting for, and he told Harry the story of the study project that had named the class and started it going under full steam.

Around Christmas time a year ago the subject of "Happy New Year" was the topic of the lesson. Mrs. Athey, the teacher, asked every member of the class to do some special study with a concordance. She told them to look up all the passages of scripture containing the words "happy" or "blessed" (for these words mean practically the same thing) and the next Sunday the class

104

would try to decide just what it is that makes a person happy. Of course, everyone wanted to be happy, and almost everyone in the class did his home work on that assignment.

On Sunday morning, with the help of Mrs. Athey, all the passages were looked up and read. There were many of them, but the class was agreed that Jesus summed it all up when he told the disciples in the upper room, "If ye know these things, happy are ye if ye do them."

It was not enough to study, or to be able to repeat scripture by heart, or even to make a fine talk about goodness. Jesus said that more important than all of this was to do good.

Mrs. Athey told the story of Albert Schweitzer, the great doctor to the black men in Africa, who said he became a doctor and a medical missionary because he wanted most of all to act for God rather than to talk about him.

That is the reason the class of third-year juniors (they were second-year juniors at the time) decided to take a name and try to live up to it. If happiness comes from doing good, then they would do all the good they could. They called themselves "hustlers" because they wanted to get busy at once and keep busy doing good every day of their lives. The Happy Hustlers prove that doing good makes people happy, for they are surely a happy as well as a busy crowd.

FROM THE
CHANGING YEAR

* * *

26

GOD'S GLORY IN A STABLE

(Christmas)

> And she gave birth to her first-born son and
> wrapped him in swaddling cloths, and laid him
> in a manger, because there was no place for
> them in the inn. —LUKE 2:7

MICHAEL was tired, very tired. In fact, during
his whole nine years it seemed that he had never been
quite so tired as now. But this was an unusual occasion,
and everyone in town was busy.

You see, the Roman emperor Augustus Caesar had
decreed that all the people in his empire should be taxed.
To make sure that none evaded this tax, he required
that each person report to the town where he was born
and where his family had lived, and there sign the register of enrollment.

Since many families had moved to other towns, and sons and daughters had married and gone to distant places, this meant journeys by great crowds of people. Of course, there were always people traveling from place to place, merchants buying and selling and people going on trips to visit their families and friends. There were also the great feast days when large groups of worshipers made pilgrimages to the temple in Jerusalem.

But this was different. There were more people traveling at the same time than ever before, and they were going in all directions. Instead of all going to Jerusalem, as at Pentecost or the Passover, they were going east and west, north and south, each to his own birthplace.

All this was exciting and would have been fun to watch, but Michael was more than a spectator. He had a job and an important one. You see, his Uncle Nathan was the keeper of the inn at Bethlehem. This was a large structure built around a courtyard. The two-story building on one side of the court was divided into a number of rooms for visitors, with a balcony running the entire length. Near the middle of this building was an archway with a large gate. Just opposite the gate, on the other side of the courtyard, was the stable section, where donkeys, cattle, and camels were cared for in stalls, while their drivers slept on the elevated platform built along the wall. In the center of the court was a well from which water was drawn for the use of the people and for the animals quartered at the inn.

Although the whole city of Bethlehem had been thronging with people all day long, the inn was probably the most crowded place in the town. Most of the families in Bethlehem were entertaining guests, for out-of-town relatives were staying with them during the time of the tax enrollment. There were many people returning to town who no longer had relatives living there. Then there were some relatives who came in such large numbers that their families did not have room for them all. So it happened that a large number of out-of-town guests found it necessary to ask for a room at the inn.

This was the reason Michael had a job. Uncle Nathan had hurried over to his house and asked his mother, Sarah, if she could spare Michael for all day and all night to work at the inn. Since Michael was glad to help Uncle Nathan, he and his constant pal Dan went back with Uncle Nathan to the inn, where both had been working hard ever since. Dan was only a shepherd dog, but he was a smart dog and was a lot of help. He did whatever Michael asked him to do, that is, if it was anything a dog could do.

So all day Michael and Dan had been running errands, drawing water from the well, carrying hay for the donkeys and camels, and helping the guests with their bundles. It was getting late now, and Michael was glad, for he wanted to eat his supper and get to bed. He was really tired. Uncle Nathan and Aunt Anna were tired too. They decided to lock up for the night, because there was no more space for guests. Every room and every nook and corner in the big house was filled with tired, sleepy travelers.

As the gate was being closed for the night, a loud knock

was heard. Nathan opened the gate, and there stood a very tired-looking man leading a donkey, upon which sat an even more tired-looking woman. The man asked for a room for the night. "If you can only find space enough for her," he said. "She is very tired and needs the rest much more than I."

Nathan hesitated, his hand on the gate. "We are overcrowded now," he said. "There is not even a corner unoccupied. I'm sorry, but there is no room."

Anna had overheard the conversation and she was now beside her husband at the gate. "Nathan," she said, "the woman is in great need of a place. We must do something. The stable is for beasts, but it is a shelter, and we can make a comfortable bed of straw there. Come, let us prepare for her at once."

The tired couple came through the gate, and Michael carried straw and helped Nathan make the bed. Then he led the donkey to the watering trough by the well, for he knew the tired animal would welcome a long cool drink. Michael was a bit afraid of camels, for they growled at him and showed their teeth, but he loved the little donkeys. So he was glad to care for this donkey and see that it had water and plenty of hay. Now, thought Michael, I can get some rest.

"One more thing, Michael," said Uncle Nathan. "I want you to be the gatekeeper tonight. The bed there is good and you can sleep well. No one should disturb you; it is late and all are tired and sound asleep. Call me if anyone knocks."

Abner, who usually watched the gate, had gone to Jericho with his family for his own enrollment.

Michael was proud to be gatekeeper. That was a man's job. Dan would sleep by his side, and with Dan he was not afraid of anything. He was too tired to take off his clothes, but he remembered to say a prayer before he lay down. Soon he was fast asleep.

Michael was awakened by a bark and a pulling at his elbow. It was hard for him to open his eyes and get to his feet. He rubbed his eyes and looked around. Dan was growling and looking toward the gate. Michael thought of his uncle and was about to run to awaken him, when he peeked through the bars and saw some shepherds standing outside. They had their crooked canes, and one was carrying a lamb. A dog was with them. Michael knew at once that there was nothing to fear.

"What do you want?" asked Michael.

"We come to see a babe born this night and announced to us by angels from heaven. He is a heavenly child, our promised Messiah."

Michael was about to say he knew of no such child, when suddenly one of the shepherds cried out, "Look, the light! He must he there!"

Sure enough, as Michael looked behind him toward the stable door, he too saw a light shining brightly. It was not the kind of light that shines from a candle or a wick soaked in oil. It was like the glow of the moon or the gleam of a star.

Michael opened the gate and followed the shepherds as they walked quietly and reverently toward the stable door. There truly was a baby lying in the manger, where hay was placed for the oxen to eat. There was music in the air and a wonderful radiance in the stable. All stood breathless and looked in awe.

After a long, long time, the elder shepherd said slowly, "Of a truth, this is the One the angels proclaimed. This is the Messiah sent from God. This is Christ the Lord."

Then the shepherds told the mother about their angel visitors, and she listened in wonder. Michael wondered too. He had often heard the story of the promised Messiah. Truly this was he. Reverently the boy knelt and, looking at the radiant face of the tiny child, he said, "My heart, my life, my all are yours, tonight—and always."

On that wonderful night in the stable at his uncle's inn, Michael learned the glorious meaning of Christmas.

27

JESUS IS REALLY ALIVE AGAIN!

(Easter)

> The Lord has risen indeed, and has appeared
> to Simon! —LUKE 24:34

REUBEN COULD NOT sleep. Bedtime was hours ago, but he was too excited even to think of sleep. How could one sleep when such unusual things were happening? How could one keep such wonderful news all to himself? Reuben jumped from his bed. Quickly he drew on his robe and ran out into the street. It was not dark, for the moon was shining brightly. Straight to the home of his chum Hiram he went. For some strange reason, although it was late, a light was shining through the window and the door was partly open. He went in without knocking.

"Reuben, why are you here at this time of night?" cried Hiram's mother in surprise. "You should have been asleep three hours ago!"

"But I just couldn't sleep," said Reuben. "Haven't you heard the news about Jesus? Did you know he is alive again?"

"What on earth do you mean, Reuben?" said Hiram's mother. "Please tell us. We knew something was happening at your Aunt Mary's house. We have seen several of Jesus' friends going in there. All seemed very excited."

"Can we wake up Hiram and tell him too?" asked Reuben. "I know he would want to know, and I just cannot wait until morning to tell him!"

Hiram's mother was eager to hear. So were Hiram's father and the friends who had come in to visit with them. They had been talking about the strange things that were going on in the neighborhood. So Hiram was awakened. He was so sleepy that he had a hard time opening his eyes and getting on his feet.

"What in the world is the matter?" he asked. "Is the house on fire, or is it an earthquake, or an enemy attack?"

"No," said Reuben, "but something so wonderful has happened that the whole world should know about it, and I wanted to tell you first of all. Jesus, who was crucified by the Roman soldiers and buried in Joseph's tomb, is alive again!"

"Please tell us all about it from the very first," said Hiram's mother. "Don't leave out one thing. We will listen."

"You know," said Reuben, "Jesus' disciples often come to my Aunt Mary's house. They meet there to pray and to talk over their plans. Aunt Mary and Cousin Mark know all of them, and they are good friends.

"Well, since Jesus was crucified, and everybody was so sorrowful, most of them have been at the house talking about this terrible thing.

"The first news came this morning. Three women had gone to the tomb of Jesus to take spices. They came back

113

here all excited and said something had happened. The big stone was rolled away from the opening of the tomb. When they went in to put spices on Jesus' body, they did not find him there. The tomb was empty. While they were standing there, wondering what to do, two men in white appeared and said, 'Why do you seek the living among the dead? Jesus is not here, but is risen as he said he would.'

"That was this morning. When disciple John and disciple Peter heard about this, they ran all the way to the tomb to see if what the women said was really the truth. They, too, have come back and told an exciting story. They found the tomb empty. They went inside and saw all the wrapping cloths there, but the body of Jesus was gone."

"Reuben, what could have happened to the body of Jesus?" asked Hiram's mother. "Were any of his disciples able to find it?"

"Let me tell the rest," said Reuben, "for I have left the most wonderful part for the last. One of the women— Mary, I think it was—stayed in the garden after the others had left. She says that Jesus actually came to her—alive —and called her by name and asked her to tell the disciples that he is risen from the dead."

"Reuben," said Hiram and his father and mother all together, "this is too wonderful to believe! Can it really be true?"

"Let me continue," said Reuben, "for there is still more. Just a while ago the friends of Jesus were meeting for prayer at my Aunt Mary's house, and two men came in breathless. They told a story as amazing as the others. They said they were walking down the road, going to Emmaus. A stranger caught up with them and walked along, talking with them about the terrible crucifixion of Jesus and the stories which the women had told about the empty tomb. They invited him to stop for dinner with them, and he did so. When he asked the blessing at the table, suddenly they knew that this stranger was Christ. Then he vanished from their sight, and they came back here as quickly as they could to tell the others they had seen the Master.

"Just a few minutes ago Jesus came right to my Aunt Mary's house. Almost all the disciples were there, praying and talking about the things that have happened today. Then—all at once—Jesus was there too! He really was. for all of them saw him and heard him speak.

"I know this is almost too strange and too wonderful to believe, but I know it is true. That is why I came here so late at night to tell Hiram and the rest of you. There is no other news like it. This makes everything different. My cousin Mark says we need not fear the Romans any more. We need not be afraid of anything any more— not even death. Jesus is able to overcome all our enemies. If we are his friends he will protect us forever!"

"Thank you, Reuben, for telling us the most important news we have ever heard in all our lives!" said Hiram's father.

"It is the good news all of us can tell to everyone we meet!" said Hiram.

115

"Yes," said Reuben, "this good news about Jesus is God's good news for the whole wide world!"

* * *

28

GIRLS AND BOYS TO THE FRONT

(Children's Day)

Let the children come to me, do not hinder them; for to such belongs the kingdom of God.
—MARK 10:14

ALL THE CHILDREN in Bethabara were excited. They had good reason to be both excited and happy. It was rumored that Jesus, the beloved teacher, was in Perea, east of the Jordon River, and was traveling southward. Possibly within a day or two he would be preaching in their town or in the wide fields along the river.

Sarah and her friend Rachel were making great plans for tomorrow.

"Let's pick a big bunch of those beautiful Star of Bethlehem flowers and give them to Jesus when we go to see him!" said Rachel.

"That is just what we must do," said Sarah, "and the very prettiest ones I ever saw are blooming down by the pond."

116

"There are some daisies there too," said Rachel, "and some nice wild lilies."

"We must get up early in the morning and pick the very prettiest of the wild flowers so we will be ready to go as soon as we hear that Jesus is coming," said Sarah.

Sarah's brother Joel was not to be left behind either. He had heard all the talk and the planning. He too wanted to see Jesus. He too wanted to take Jesus a present. He knew just what it would be. Up on the little hill back of their town was a grove of trees. There he and his friends had found one wild date tree that bore the sweetest of fruit.

"I know what I'll do," said Joel to himself. I'll go over to David's house right now and get him to help me get some of those wild dates for Jesus."

So night came and morning followed, and there was the sound of glad voices all over the town of Bethabara. Boys and girls were all getting ready to go to meet Jesus, the great teacher.

No one knew if he actually would come to Bethabara, but all hoped he would pay their town a visit.

Then it happened. A traveler arrived in Bethabara and spread the news—"Jesus is coming this way!"

What a welcome was prepared for Jesus! The children were most eager. They ran down the road to be the first to see him and greet him.

And then he came. It was too wonderful for words. Here in their own country was Jesus, the man sent of God, who loved everyone and spoke words of comfort and good cheer. It was said that he healed the sick, and

117

caused the cripples to walk and the blind to see. He told his messages in interesting parables which all could remember.

There was no formal welcoming. Jesus did not seem to want any special attention paid to him. As the crowd gathered he just began talking to them, and they drew closer and closer so they would not miss a single word.

Sarah and Rachel, with their wild flowers, and Joel and David, with their sweet dates for Jesus, were just a few of the crowd of children who had come to see the great teacher. In fact, everyone in town was there! As they tried to get up front so they could see, they heard one of the men who stood near Jesus speak rather harshly to a woman who was holding out her child toward Jesus, asking his blessing.

"Stand back," said the man. "The Master is too busy to deal with babies and children. He is here to teach men wisdom and proclaim the will of the Almighty."

"But could we not have one word with the Teacher?" insisted the mother with the small child. "His blessing would mean so much to our child and to our home!"

Before the man near Jesus could answer, Jesus himself came forward and took the little child from the mother's arms and smiled upon him as he said to all the people: "Let the children come to me, do not hinder them; for to such belongs the kingdom of God. Truly, I say to you, whoever does not receive the kingdom of God like a child shall not enter it."

Then the people up front made way for the children, and they came from all directions—right up where Jesus was. Sarah and Rachel brought him their flowers; Joel and David brought their dates; and Jesus thanked them and asked all the children to gather close around him so he could talk to them. As he smiled upon them and talked it seemed that he forgot that all the other people were there, for he made a little circle just for the children.

The day Jesus came to Bethabara was the greatest day any of the people of that town had ever known. But it seemed most wonderful to the children; never before had anyone been so kind to them. Never before had anyone taken time to talk just to them alone. Never before had they met a person who made them feel good just to be near him.

Sarah and Rachel, Joel and David, never forgot that day. Children all over the world never forget the day they meet Jesus, the great lover of all children everywhere.

* * *

29

THINK! AND BE THANKFUL

(Thanksgiving)

> *Bless the Lord, O my soul, and forget not all his benefits.* —PS. 103:2

RONNIE was feeling very low. Even though it was the day before Thanksgiving he was not in a thankful mood. It seemed as though the very bottom of his world had dropped out.

The trouble had begun just two weeks ago when Ronnie's best friend Charlie brought him the bad news. Charlie's father was being promoted by his company, and that meant a move to a larger city, where he was to be manager of a branch office. Of course this meant a great deal to Charlie's father, but it was a blow to Charlie and to Ronnie. They were such close friends and were together almost all the time. If Charlie was not at Ronnie's house, then Ronnie was at Charlie's. They played together, they studied together, they went on trips together, they ate together, and they often slept together.

Furthermore, they had made some big plans for the winter—basketball, skating, hiking, ice fishing, and a lot more. Ronnie and Charlie couldn't imagine any of these sports being fun unless they were going to enjoy them together.

The boys walked home from school very slowly. They had only a few hours left to talk things over. Charlie's father was taking the family away that very evening. He had to be on his new job by Monday morning. The Thanksgiving vacation gave the family just enough time to move and get located in their new home.

That was a sad night for Ronnie. At the supper table he did not want anything to eat. He had nothing to say. He was really blue.

"Ronnie, you must eat something," said his mother. "You mustn't take Charlie's leaving so hard. He is only moving to Detroit, and that isn't very far. You will get

120

to see him often. We will drive over there, and they will drive over here."

"But we can only see each other once in a while," sobbed Ronnie. "I want to see Charlie every day. I don't see why Mr. Bender had to take that new job anyway. He should have thought about Charlie and me."

Ronnie's mother and father both tried to cheer him up, but he couldn't even smile. As he left the table he said, "This isn't going to be any Thanksgiving for me. I haven't a thing to be thankful for!"

Ronnie was not interested in television or in talking with the rest of the family. He went to bed early, for he couldn't think of anything he wanted to do. He kept saying to himself, "I haven't a thing to be thankful for. This is no Thanksgiving Day for me."

After what seemed a long, long night, Ronnie found himself sitting at the breakfast table, but all was different. There was no orange juice, no milk, no cereal, no toast. His father and mother and his sister were not there either. All he saw was a bare table with a crust of dry bread at his place and a tin cup of water. He tried to eat but wasn't hungry.

"Well, I'll go up to my room and get out some of my things," he said to himself. "With a day off I can practice throwing baskets with my basketball. I want to work that new jigsaw puzzle and take a look at the comic books Daddy brought me when he came home from Cincinnati."

Ronnie climbed the stairs slowly. The place was so quiet. No one seemed to be in the house. Where was

Mother and where were Dad and sister Sue? They must be sleeping late because it was a holiday.

Ronnie went to get his basketball. It was not there! He found an old "dead" tennis ball, but the basketball was nowhere to be found. In fact, the jigsaw puzzle was gone too and the new comic books. Everything that should have been on that shelf was gone! The closet was bare and dusty. What had happened? Had someone stolen all Ronnie's things?

Ronnie rushed to his father and mother's room. They were not there! He hurried to his sister's room to ask if she knew where Father and Mother had gone. Sue was gone too!

This was too much for Ronnie. He couldn't hold back the tears. He was so broken up over his terrible loss he shook the bed with his moans of grief. And the shaking awakened him—for Ronnie was asleep and having a horrible dream. When he opened his eyes he realized that it was morning and that his world was still there. He jumped out of bed and ran into his parents' room with a shout loud enough to awaken the whole neighborhood.

"What on earth is the matter with you, Ronnie?" asked his father.

"There's nothing the matter with me now," said Ronnie. "Last night I thought I didn't have a thing to be thankful for, but today I really have. This is going to be the greatest Thanksgiving Day I ever knew in my whole life!"

At the big Thanksgiving dinner that day, Father asked Ronnie to read the devotional for the day, and he read with real understanding, "Bless the Lord, O my soul, and forget not all his benefits."

* * *

30

TALKING AND DOING

(Halloween)

> A man had two sons; and he went to the first and said, "Son, go and work in the vineyard today." And he answered, "I will not"; but afterward he repented and went. And he went to the second and said the same; and he answered, "I go, sir," but did not go. Which of the two did the will of his father?
>
> —MATT. 21:28-31

THE BOYS AND girls were making plans for Halloween. They had been talking about the fun of collecting coins for the United Nations Children's Fund, which also is called UNICEF, and providing a treat for boys and girls of distant lands who need food and clothing.

"How many of you will take these UNICEF boxes and collect coins?" asked the teacher.

Up went hands all over the room.

"Do any of you have ideas as to how you will use them?" asked the teacher.

123

"Mary and I are going to visit every house in our block," said Jane, "and I am sure we will fill our boxes with coins."

"John, Jim, and I are going to do something extra special," said Bill. "We are going to dress in Indian costumes and do a fancy dance on each neighbor's porch. They will be glad to pay us for our fine performance."

"Our gang is going to sing songs as we do at Christmas time," said Sally. "We are sure people will be glad to hear us, and we will tell them all about UNICEF and get lots of money." *United Nations Children's Fund.*

One by one, the boys and girls told of their plans to go from door to door on Halloween to collect money for the boys and girls of other lands. But one boy had nothing to say. He did not hold up his hand, and he did not tell how he expected to collect his money. It seemed that he was not very much interested in the project.

"Sam," said the teacher, "aren't you going to join us in this Halloween game?"

"I'm thinking about it," said Sam.

"But don't you know it will be lots of fun, and don't you have some plans?" asked the teacher

"Not exactly," said Sam, "but I'm thinking about it."

Halloween came, and boys and girls all over the city were having fun at parties and going on tours of the neighborhood.

The next morning at school the UNICEF boxes were to be returned and the money counted to see how much the class had raised for children overseas. Many of the children brought their boxes, and all reported a good

124

time. Some had only a few pennies in their boxes, and the class was disappointed with the small amount, for they had expected to raise a large sum.

When the teacher asked how the various plans had turned out, she was surprised at the answers. Mary and Jane had not carried out their plan of visiting every house, because Jane's father had taken them to the show and when they got back it was too late to go calling.

Bill had been unable to get the Indian costumes he had expected to use, so he and John and Jim just went out on "trick or treat" in the old way and collected candy and apples for themselves. They were really ashamed. It would have been much better to do what they had planned.

Sally did get a few to go with her to sing, but when they got to Esther's house, she invited them in and they called up some other girls and had a party. They did not make any more calls.

Sam listened to all these reports but did not say a thing. Finally, the teacher called for his report.

Sam walked up to the teacher's desk and set down his UNICEF carton. It sounded full of coins. Everyone watched as the teacher opened it and poured the coins on the desk. What a pile they made! When the money was counted, it was found to amount to $10.65.

Actually, Sam collected more money than all the rest of the class together. When the teacher asked him how he was able to get so much, he simply said, "I made a list of all the people I know in my neighborhood. I called them up two or three days ago and told them all about

UNICEF. They seemed to like the idea. Then I told them to be ready when I made my visits, and it was no trouble at all to fill my carton."

The teacher said quietly, "There was a lot of talking in this room the other day when we planned this project. Sam did not have much to say. It looks to me like doing raises more money than talking."

I wonder who in this story did what their teacher would have wanted to be done? Sam It sounds to me as though he did more thinking as to how he might collect, + was a little more serious about it. The other boys + girls had made plans, which would have been alright + they probably would have made collections like Sam, but it seems to me they forgot about the importance of their work + when the time came they were more concerned about themselves and having fun. I'm pretty sure the teacher was quite disappointed in the majority of the class.

126

There are times we make vows or promises to God, our heavenly father, and we become careless and break our promises, When we ask forgiveness, thru our prayers - God does forgive - but I wonder how God feels when we make the same mistakes over & over. I imagine He gets